Present by Larry

LeRoy Helmuth

C  F

THE
WINGLESS
CROW

ESSAYS FROM THE
"THORNAPPLES" COLUMN BY

CHARLES FERGUS

THE PENNSYLVANIA GAME COMMISSION, PUBLISHER
HARRISBURG, PENNSYLVANIA

All of the essays originally appeared in *Pennsylvania Game News* magazine,
with the exception of "Lord and Master of June," which was first printed in
Science 82 and is used here by permission. The epigraph is from the poem
"Talking About Birds," translated from the Vietnamese by John Balaban.

ACKNOWLEDGMENTS: I thank my wife, Nancy Marie Brown,
for reading the manuscript and offering many valuable sugges-
tions and comments. I thank my teacher, S. Leonard Rubinstein,
for recognizing the theme and urging me to arrange the essays
around it. And I thank Bob Bell, friend and editor, without
whose support, guidance, and encouragement this book would
not exist. —CF

Book design by the author

FOR MY MOTHER AND FATHER

CONTENTS

CONTENTS

The Crows, now, are really just like us, cawing
From far off, 'Wash up. The journey's over.'
Vietnamese folk poem

THE WINGLESS CROW

Stump-Sitting

I went stump-sitting the other day. I walked up the mountain, stopped at the first good stump I came to, and set myself down. I had no idea what I would see. Maybe a porcupine, an old gray-faced buck, or a hawk. Maybe nothing.

Well, not quite nothing. A dirty-white mushroom pokes its snout through the leaves. It looks like *Lactarius piperatus,* a mushroom the settlers used to dry and grind up and sprinkle on their deer chops as a kind of pepper. I start to go check, but stop myself. Against the rules. When you're stump-sitting, you have to stick to your stump.

I look around, taking stock. Tall oaks—red, white, and chestnut oaks—still green. Hickories waving yellow leaves. Dead leaves underfoot, a brown carpet interrupted by green shoots, bent and waiting for frost. Purple asters, yellow goldenrod, and white snakeroot, the last flowers of the year. I close my eyes and listen. From the valley drift sounds: dogs barking, a rooster crowing, crows cawing, cows, bells, a tractor, a door slamming, a hammer, a woman calling. Here on the mountain, a sound like the whispered word "rust." I open my eyes. Another leaf swings down and joins the carpet.

A tan moth flutters past. It flies in aimless haste, colliding softly with stems, leaves, and a grapevine. It circles my post and flits away. A crane fly lands on my knee, flails its wand-like legs, departs. A crow slips over the treetops, discussing matters with itself.

A small bumblebee swings on a yellow frond of goldenrod. I stick my nose within a couple of inches and watch the bee stab each tiny star-shaped flower with a pointed red tongue. The hum, when the insect flies up the stem, sounds loud as a trailbike.

I know a little about bumblebees. This worker, for instance, will not survive past fall. Young, fertilized queens are the only members of a colony to make it through the winter. In early spring, a queen emerges from hibernation, sips a drink of nectar from a flower, and lumbers off in search of a nest. An abandoned vole's lair, dark and full of dry grasses, will do nicely. The queen provisions her new home with pollen and nectar, and starts laying eggs.

Since there never seem to be enough nest sites to go around, another queen bumblebee will usually try to oust the first. They fight viciously with their stingers. Eight dead queens have been found at a single nest entrance. A victorious invader will usually accept the first queen's brood, and if the combatants were of different species, the resulting colony will have two different types of worker bees. The workers get along peaceably enough; all have the same colony smell, even though their black-and-yellow markings differ.

A nattering comes from above.

A nuthatch bobs headfirst down a tree, sounding its nasal *yank yank*. The call has always seemed to me the muttering of a simpleton. The bird spirals out a branch, preening it of insect eggs and spiders. A simply but impeccably dressed bird in white bib, gray suit, and black cap. Soon the nuthatch is joined by three more of its breed, two downy woodpeckers, a couple of tufted titmice, and six or eight chickadees. Birdwatchers call such a convocation a mixed flock, and offer explanations for the unusual socializing: It thwarts predators. More eyes find more food. The birds just like to hang around together.

The chickadees are the talkers in the bunch. They keep the flock together with a soft, high *tseet* call, and with a call that sounds like their name. If stump-sitting rules permitted, I might follow this band around its feeding circuit of perhaps twenty acres. If a neigh-

4

boring flock dared trespass, my chickadees would chase away the intruders, calling a strident *deedeedeedee* or *chebeche*. Once the boundary dispute was settled, the flock would return to feeding, and the *tseet* call would dominate the conversation once again.

As the birds feed around me, I spot a flashy dresser among the bankers' suits: a black-throated blue warbler. Unlike the regulars in the flock, who stay at home year-round, the warbler winters in the Caribbean. As it passes south, it likes to hook up with resident mixed flocks, apparently realizing that the local birds know the best feeding sites. I appreciate the philosophy. When on the road I always eat at cafés whose parking lots are filled with battered pick-up trucks.

The flock moves on. I stretch and stamp my feet, lean out and look at my stump. A foot and a half across, no bark, dark brown laced with yellow mold. It is made passing comfortable by a square of sheepskin that, miraculously, has traveled with me on Western backpacking trips and Pennsylvania deer hunts and has never been left behind. Between my feet is another stumpsitter's accessory, a Canadian army field engineer's pack. The gift of a naturalist friend, the pack is kept hanging by its strap from the doorknob in my study, and slung over my shoulder whenever I go out. The main compartment holds three field guides. Outside pockets accommodate a compass, mirror, whistle, knife, matches, notebook, pencil, pill bottle, and hand lens.

I fish out the lens. Leaning to a tree, I look for what the nuthatch seeks. If the gray, ridged bark conceals anything edible, I cannot find it. But there are lichens, gray-green crenulated splotches the size of half dollars.

Lichens are the toughest plants that grow. Peel one off a tree, dry it for ten years, give it a drink of water, and watch it spring back to life. A lichen is two organisms in one: an alga and a fungus. The alga can live by itself, but the fungus cannot survive without its companion. The alga grows in the tissue of the fungus, gaining moisture, protection, and minerals, and passing food to its host. Lichens on trees shrink into the bark, living on water, air,

5

and traces of minerals in rain and dew. Lichens on stone exude acid to leach out minerals, which the plants consume. Lichens expand when they soak up water, contract when they dry; like freezing and thawing, this cycling breaks a stone down bit by bit.

A loud beating close by my ear makes me flinch, scaring off a bird that had just landed on the brim of my hat. The bird, a wren, flits to a low bush. Tail straight up in the air, it churrs at me.

It occurs to me that stumps would be excellent places to ensconce certain people. Politicians, for instance. They would get a chance to peek at a small segment of nature. They might learn humility by getting scolded, by having midges fly in their noses, and by getting rained and snowed on. They might see a flower or a sunset. They would be kept out of trouble, and they might even enjoy it.

Maybe we should draft a law requiring everyone to sit on a stump at least one day a year. It would be a civic obligation, like jury duty. It would be therapeutic, a societal authorization to do nothing. Of course, there wouldn't be enough stumps to go around. Legitimate substitutes would include logs, rocks, streambanks, mountaintops, and the lower branches of trees. The number one rule, however, would remain in force: Stick to your stump.

A chipmunk races down a fallen log. He vanishes in a grapevine, a tangle of whiskery bark, red tendrils, yellow leaves. He resurfaces and begins wrestling with a bunch of grapes, his movements, like the wren's, jerky but precise. I move a hand, and he dashes beneath a leaf. He chirps steadily at me, cheeks collapsing and tail flicking with every call. Finally he darts behind the log.

I blow on my hands, ram them into my pockets, and look out into the forest. A creeper twists around a sapling. An oak gall lies like a broken brown egg. A yellow fern flags in the breeze. Red pulp of berries, opened by the chickadees for the seeds inside, litters the ground under a dogwood.

I remember stump-sittings past. Once, a Cooper's hawk flashed by, wings pumping, head swiveling, body juking past the tree trunks; I caught sight of his eye, red above the hooked beak. One summer evening, a deer came so close that I could see its whiskered muzzle, flies on its eyelashes, its lower jaw working side to side. I scarcely breathed. When it hit my scent, it whirled and sprinted through the trees. Another time a porcupine, mewling softly and with porcupette in tow, waddled past my boot. When I stamped the ground, its yellow quills bristled.

Today, no porcupine, no deer, no hunting hawk.

A goldenrod nods against my leg. I pluck the top frond. Something among the flowers catches my eye: a purple, ringed knob like a tiny bermuda onion. I open it with my thumbnail. Inside is a headless, orange maggot the size of a grain of rice. Exposed to the chill, it accordians in my palm. I collect two more of the larval cases, storing them in the pill bottle to take home for identifying.

I stand and shoulder the field pack. Looking around the woods, I am reminded of a quote from the scientist Louis Agassiz. ''I spent the summer traveling,'' he said. ''I got halfway across my backyard.''

On Being a Curmudgeon

A friend sent me to the dictionary: He called me a curmudgeon. I had a good idea what the word meant, but I wanted to be sure. A curmudgeon, I read, is a cantankerous person.

Curmudgeon is one of those words, like bowdlerize and bugbear and ululation, that is rich and delightfully descriptive and yet is not used very often. The last place I saw it in print was in an article by John McPhee. The subject was the New Jersey Pine Barrens, and McPhee was explaining his thoughts about adding photographs to his text. He called himself "a curmudgeon with few deep beliefs, one of which [is] that a single word is worth at least a thousand pictures."

The origin of curmudgeon is obscure. It has an Anglo Saxon ring to it. It sounds like a cross between cur and bludgeon. I have always felt that it implied a person who was, in addition to being cantankerous, in exceedingly secure possession of his beliefs. I know a few curmudgeons. One was a Wyoming rancher, who had been, over the course of his career, a muleskinner, a big-game guide, and a breaker of horses. Once, in the thirties, he skied fifty miles from his homestead in the Absaroka Mountains to a bank in town, to make a monthly payment on a loan. The snows were deep, and the mail was not running; the round trip took three days.

This man was of the certain opinion that drinking glacial melt—water that had melted off a glacier—would make a person weak, or, as he put it, puny. I wanted to know why. Was it the ground-up rock in the water? The water's coldness? Drinking too fast? I asked a lot of questions. He could offer no technical explanation. Finally he fixed his eyes on me—the irises were dark brown, and I could see the whites all around them—and said, in a voice somewhat louder and higher than normal, "That's just the way it is."

I am trying, now, to remember the context in which my friend called me a curmudgeon. I believe we were talking about television. The last time I shared space with a TV was three years ago. I had bought an old black-and-white set at a yard sale. Where I lived, I could get two channels. I watched a little football and baseball, and the news, and sometimes, if I was too tired to read or to do anything useful, I would turn on the set and absorb whatever happened to be there. I always felt guilty afterwards. There are so many good books to read, so many stories to write, that to sit passively seemed a sin.

The TV became ill on one occasion and refused to work; I had it cured. A month later, it went on the fritz again. I decided to get rid of it. I thought about taking it for a long walk down the fence-row and putting it out of its misery with my revolver, but I didn't want to leave a mess. So I disconnected it and lugged it out to the truck, drove into town, and found a Dempster Dumpmaster. I climbed into the bed of the truck, hoisted the set onto my shoulder, and pushed it over the brink. A dull crump issued from inside. A pedestrian stared, then snapped his head away.

Now, when someone mentions television, I can play dumb. "Dan Rather? Never heard of him."

I also do not believe in pole lights. Pole lights are those blindingly bright lights that people affix to poles next to their houses. Drive down any rural road and you will see them, blotting out the stars and turning the dark into half-light and shadow. I've never seen anybody out working under one. Besides wasting electricity, they are among the most impertinent of inventions. If I had a device that could disable every pole light in the country, I'd use it.

At one time I lived on a farm along a busy highway. I grew more or less accustomed to the traffic; it was like a river flowing past my door. Out front, along the road, stood a billboard. One night when I went to bed, an unfamiliar glare penetrated the room. I looked outside. The lights on the billboard were on. One of them, slightly askew, pointed directly at my window. I had lived in the house for five years, and the billboard lights had never been on, until now.

My throat constricted. I lay in bed and fantasized about what I might do. Saw down the billboard. Saw its legs three-quarters of the way through and wait for a storm to push it over. Set it on fire. Shoot out the lights. Finally I dressed and went outside. A wooden box hung on one of the billboard's legs. The box had a door, which I opened. Inside was a switch. I tripped it, and the lights went dead.

A week later, they were on again. I flipped the switch. In three days they were back. I turned them off. The next time the lights were on, someone had nailed the box shut. I pried the box open, turned off the lights, and nailed the door shut with bigger nails. The sign stayed dark for a month. One night, a wind came up and stripped the wood from its frame. No one replaced it.

Not far from where I lived back then, there is a true curmudgeon in residence. He has sturdy opinions about rattlesnakes, Japanese beetles, gypsy moths, marauding house cats, and the worth and wisdom of government officials. My curmudgeonly friend is retired and presumably on a fixed income. He hikes, hunts, and fishes with the freezer preeminent in his mind. He is always coming home with a basket of mushrooms, a sack of nuts, a bucket of berries. He devotes a large portion of each winter to ice-fishing. In ice-fishing, one stands on a frozen lake and dangles a hook through a hole in the ice, hoping a fish will bite; a curmudgeon's pastime if ever there was one.

My friend will not suffer abuse. Denied courteous service in a store, he is apt to raise his voice, alerting other customers. In this wise he reminds me of my maternal great-grandfather, Mose

Grecian, a wiry Kansan who is reputed to have reached through the window bars of an impertinent bank teller's booth, seized the man by the collar, lifted him from his seat, and, while explaining the importance of civility, impressed the man's face into the grill.

Great-grandfather was a farmer, and farmers, I would say, stand in great peril of becoming curmudgeons. Writers and editors are often curmudgeons. Carpenters can be exceedingly fine curmudgeons. Part of the reason may be economic; in all of these trades one sweats and strains—with words, or implements, or tools—and rarely, if ever, makes much money. I have never met a stockbroker or an accountant or an insurance salesman who was a curmudgeon. Dentists and doctors are almost automatically excluded from the society, although veterinarians, particularly those who practice on large animals, often belong. I have met more male curmudgeons than female; women seem more sensible, more accepting, more capable of adjusting to situations where curmudgeons would rather grumble and grouch.

A curmudgeon is intractable, adament, opinionated, outspoken, and set aside from the normal mass of humanity. A true curmudgeon, though, does not forget his ties to mankind. When Great-grandfather dented the teller's forehead, he was making the point that all men deserve courtesy and respect. Most curmudgeons retain the ability to laugh at themselves; they don't take anybody too seriously.

I've always had a notion that animals could be curmudgeons, too. A gunsmith friend who is a curmudgeon has a squirrel dog who is a curmudgeon, and a ram who is also one. (Anybody in the business of raising sheep and repairing guns is actually a double curmudgeon: Only rarely does either profession pay good money, and both would try the patience of Job.) Once I saw my friend walk past his ram, who was eyeing him with head lowered. My friend leapt into the air and, with the side of his shoe, clobbered the beast squarely between the eyes. When two curmudgeons get together, watch out.

Among animals, ravens are curmudgeons. So are crows and, to a

11

lesser extent, blue jays. Badgers are most certainly curmudgeons, although I've never known one well enough to say. Of the three little pigs, the third was the curmudgeon. Anyone who would build anything of stone has a curmudgeonly streak in him. Stone masonry is tedious, hard on the hands and back, the most individual of ventures. Naturally, I am bound and determined to case my house with stone: I have, over the last several years, disassembled several barn and house foundations to get good ones.

It's hard for me to pass up a stone. If, when hiking, I find a potential building stone, I'll carry it a mile. A friend and I once transported a stone that is eight inches thick by eighteen inches wide by six feet long. It was a stoop on a barn. It will be my front door stoop. We calculated it to weigh a thousand pounds.

Last fall I was walking in the woods when I came upon fifty or so stones that had been ranked between two trees. Their rectangular shapes and dressed, weathered faces bespoke tenure in a wall. I found the closest farmhouse and knocked.

A man with white hair and crooked glasses answered the door and promptly asked me in. He made me a cup of tea, settled back in a rocking chair, and regarded me with hazy eyes. He had a small black puppy, which attacked my fist until I petted it.

I inquired about the stones.

"Oh, them," he said. "I'd like to let you have 'em, but I can't." He began to rock. "Might need 'em. Been thinkin' about buildin' a place back on the mountain. Good stones is hard to find."

I agreed. I told him about the house I was planning, and waited for him to change his mind; he looked about eighty.

He leaned forward in the chair. "Look out that window," he commanded.

I followed his finger.

"See that apple tree?" he said. "I grafted it when I was a little squirt. It still bears fruit. People don't know how to graft anymore. You know how to graft?"

I shook my head.

"One day I was up in that tree pruning. I heard this sound in the sky and looked up. Dang near fell out of the tree. It was an airplane. First airplane I ever seen."

The old man called the puppy. I knew, then, that I wasn't going to get the stones. I wasn't going to get out of the farmhouse for a while, either. He was a curmudgeon, that old man, and he had me good and proper.

Paper Traveling

Some people study the classifieds. Others scour star charts, seed brochures, or sporting goods catalogs. I look at topographic maps.

A topographic map, or topo, is a visual representation of a chunk of land, depicting a wide range of geographic and man-made features. Depending on local relief and vegetation, a topo can be a work of art worth hanging on your wall. Often it is a lively document of local culture and history. Topos are useful to hunters, fishermen, foragers, birdwatchers, backpackers, loggers, miners, land planners—to anyone interested in anything outdoors.

Topos of the 7½-minute series, the most useful line, sell for $2.25. Like everything else, they've felt inflation's squeeze; in 1937 they cost a dime. But even at today's price, a topo remains one of the few authentic bargains a person can latch onto.

I own dozens of topos and am constantly buying new ones. The maps, folded in green-and-white rectangles, are wedged into a bookshelf beside a row of blue-jacketed field guides. Both maps and guides impart a sense of massed practicality, like ranked firewood or rows of home-canned vegetables. But the topos do more: They fire my imagination with their powers of transport.

Considerable history lies behind these beautiful, detailed maps. In the 1860s and 1870s, four separate expeditions were receiving federal funds to map portions of the American West. Lieutenant George Wheeler was knocking about the Southwest, surveying lands appropriated from Mexico two decades earlier. John Wesley

14

Powell (he would become the first white man to lead an expedition through the Grand Canyon) was charting the convoluted Colorado Plateau. Clarence King was mapping eastward from California. And Ferdinand Hayden (the famous valley in Yellowstone Park is named after him) was scouting Nebraska, the Dakotas, and Wyoming. As might be expected, competition sprang up, causing squabbles, delays, duplications. In 1879 a fed-up Congress threw water on the combatants with an Act creating—guess what—a new federal agency. They called it the Geological Survey.

The Survey, based in the Department of the Interior, has for the last century conducted geological research, inventoried water resources, overseen mineral development on federal lands, and, of course, made maps. All kinds of maps. Maps of volcanoes, maps of Mars, maps of degree days, air pollution, sunshine, rainfall, tides, zip codes, divorce rates, dentists per one hundred thousand population, and even maps of topographic mapping progress.

Although fascinating, most of these maps have limited utility for outdoor enthusiasts. More useful are two sets of topographic maps, the 15-minute and 7½-minute series, which together cover some 86 percent of the United States. About 65 percent of the nation has been reduced to the 7½-minute maps; if the whole country were mapped and the sheets laid out all together, they would cover five acres. Maps of the 15-minute series represent plots of land 15 minutes of latitude by 15 minutes of longitude. Their scale is one map unit to 62,500 land units, or approximately one inch to one mile. The 7½s are more detailed, covering 7½ minutes of latitude by 7½ of longitude, with one inch equaling two thousand feet.

In compiling a topographic map (also called a quadrangle, or simply a quad), cartographers use aerial photographs, stereoscopic plotting instruments, and field data to locate a cornucopia of detail. Various symbols and colors represent woodlands, orchards, marshes, dunes, glaciers, rivers, rapids, intermittent streams, springs, waterfalls, and many other terrain features. In rural areas, individual buildings show up as tiny black squares; cities and towns get a pink wash. The maps show dams, schools, churches, oil tanks, gas lines, quarries, shipwrecks, railroads, highways, logging trails, footpaths, and scads of other additions, including the imaginary lines—township, municipal, county, state, and so on—that people assign to the earth.

Topos also capture verticality. Thin brown contour lines overlie a map like the whorls of a fingerprint. On a 7½, each line stands for twenty feet of elevation. With a little practice, the eye can scan a sheet and see cliffs, canyons, flats, rolling hills, mountains.

All this detail would be worse than useless if it weren't accurate; prospectors might snoop in the wrong places, hikers blunder off cliffs, and fishermen cast their lines in briar patches. In 1941, the Geological Survey adopted standards for the 7½-minute series requiring 90 percent of all points to achieve one-fiftieth of an inch accuracy tolerance. Translated to the landscape, this means that the streamside bench you pick as an ideal campsite will be within forty feet of where the map says it is. Spot checks have shown that most Survey maps are much more precise than the rules require.

They are plenty accurate for my standards, and on more than one occasion they have kept me from getting lost, or at least inconveniently delayed outside the bounds of civilization. Topos have also helped me find prospective morel patches, deer crossings, cliffs where bobcats might den, streams harboring herpetological oddities, solitude, skinny-dipping ponds, and, although I didn't trust the technique at first, grouse and woodcock.

One of my friends approaches upland bird hunting scientifically. Several years ago he bought all the quadrangles for the area we hunt. He took a red pencil and circled a dozen or so white patches that interrupted the green woodland overlay. "Reverting fields," he announced. "Aspen, hawthorn, raspberry, grapes. Good grouse food." He circled zones of green stippling in forests far from any road. "Abandoned orchards." He marked off a flat the creek bent around. "Just the kind of place a flight woodcock would pitch into."

16

I snorted. "Grouse are where you find 'em. And I don't think a woodcock would land there. Looks too swampy."

We tested his deductions the first week of season. We found hawthorn thick enough to trip turtles. Aspen, raspberry, black locusts hung with grapes, tired apple trees. And, probably because each blank spot on the map was a good half-hour's walk from the nearest road, few hunters. Grouse? In number. Surpassed, however, by woodcock loafing in alder stands thick as bamboo groves that we reached by donning hip boots, slogging across mud flats, and wading swollen creeks.

I began ordering quadrangles by the dozen.

Another friend demonstrated how to fold my maps, delivering me from interminable wrestling with sheets that insist on returning to tubular form, the way the Geological Survey mails them to you. Here's how to do it. Unroll your map face up, with north at the top of the sheet. Pick up the right edge of the map and fold it over even with the left. Fold each half back on itself. You now have a tall, narrow sheet four layers thick. Pick up the sheet and fold the top half down. Fold each resulting half up to form an accordioned rectangle 5½ by 6½ inches, with the quadrangle name presented on the front and the back. Don't worry if you don't get it perfect. Anything beats the perpetual tube.

That same friend taught me a handy formula for estimating rate-of-travel on trails marked on 7½s. Assume a fifty-pound backpack, uneven terrain, and a fair state of physical fitness. (The first two, at least, are practically givens for an extended Rocky Mountain trek, like the one I was on when taught this technique.) Start with a base rate of two miles per hour. For every thousand feet you must climb, add another hour. Example: If your route covers eight miles and ascends from eight thousand to ten thousand feet, figure on walking six hours. Add an extra hour for breaks and stream crossings, more if you have to ford in late afternoon when the streams run full of the day's snowmelt.

Although a two-thousand-foot climb would be rare in Pennsylvania, the formula works here, too. But don't go without topos just because you're not climbing high or traveling far. Topos alert you to turns in the trail, cabins, shelters, vistas, springs, and hidden hollows. They are also great entertainment. I read them on breaks while hiking, or at home, or in the local library's map room. I pull out quads at random, or because their names intrigue me: White Pine, Lee Fire Tower, Cyclone, Burnt Cabins, Bear Knob. Place names on the maps ring with a simple, descriptive charm. Thick Mountain. Hickory Swale. Tumbling Run. Shade Gap. The Winehead. Spechty Kopf. Ganderstep Knob. You wouldn't believe all the Laurel and Trout runs carving Pennsylvania; bear, deer, and turkey names also abound. Panther Hollow, Wolf Run, Elk Fork, and Buffalo Gap enshrine a vanished wilderness, as do Indian names that fairly flow off the tongue: Susquehanna, Sinnemahoning, Mahantango, Moshannon.

Plenty of Indian names decorate my Wyoming quads, souvenirs of four backpacking trips in that state. I've camped or hiked on Papoose Creek, Squaw Peak, Teepee Creek, and Dead Indian Meadows in the Absaroka Range. Absaroka is itself a Crow Indian word; it means "sparrowhawk," the name that the tribe called itself.

My maps are grimy and pack-chafed, stained with tea and sweat, their edges imprinted with Vibram lugs (you have to hold a quad down to read it in a blow); scrawled on their blank sides are menus and equipment lists. Every time I unfold one, I see the places I have been. Hurricane Mesa, where clouds raced in to blast the broad, flat uplift with lightning, driving us down to timberline. Tourist Creek, where two full-curl bighorn rams watched us descend. Beaver Park, where Randy spilled the butterscotch pudding. Wells Creek, where the only path was the creek itself, falling out of a notch in the mountain and freezing on the boulders below; where we looked at the map and scratched our heads and wondered if we'd make it without ropes. We did.

Topos remind me of the treasure maps we drew as kids. Only the treasures of the quadrangles are real, here and now, dwindling yet still attainable, the richest treasures we will ever see.

18

A Four-Star Shower

Terry Dunkle and I recline on lawn chairs in the middle of a field. He is wearing a watch cap and a down jacket. I have on two wool shirts and a down vest. I am not quite warm, even though it is the twelfth of August.

"New moon, low humidity, no clouds," Terry says. "You don't often get to watch the Perseids with the sky this dark and clear."

A bat flits through the deepening blue. Over the mountain, the Big Dipper has begun to twinkle. The field we have chosen for our vigil is a ten acre weed patch on the south slope of the Allegheny Front, a northeast-to-southwest prominence separating the Allegheny Plateau from the ridge-and-valley region of Pennsylvania. On all sides, trees wall us in. A barred owl hoots from the woods; a second owl answers.

Stars are popping out all over the sky. Terry points to a cluster of five, shaped like a tilted W. "That's Cassiopeia. And up there" (he points straight up) "is Vega—brightest star in the summer sky." Terry calls out more stars and constellations, but my gaze keeps returning northeast, the direction our lawn chairs point, the direction from which the Perseids will come.

The first meteor flashes across the sky, a white streak that glows half a second before fading.

An instant later a second meteor shoots out of the North Star, longer and brighter than the first, with a red glow to its tail.

19

During supper, Terry had filled me in on these silent fireworks. The Perseids are ice and dust from a comet that broke apart thousands of years ago. The particles, most no larger than an elderberry, float in a band around the sun. Each year in August the earth's orbit takes it through the band. The dust and ice strike our planet's atmosphere at a closing speed of forty miles per second, and friction burns them up. We see the fiery collisions.

Terry takes off his glasses and polishes away dew. Terry is thirty-one years old. He teaches writing at a nearby university and writes articles for magazines. He loves to explore detail: why leaves have their characteristic shapes, how a sidewinder slips over sand, how a celestial dust band changed the earth's climate eons in the past.

Now it is dark, and the Perseids come fast and furious. Perseids are classed as shower meteors because they fall in concentrated numbers during a short period of time. If two observers sit back to back, each will see over sixty per hour during the shower peak on August 12, a few less in the weeks immediately before and after. Swifter and brighter than most other meteors, the Perseids can be seen from anywhere on earth. Terry watched them from the banks of Pine Creek in upstate Pennsylvania, where he grew up. His grandfather saw the same shower from the trenches in World War I.

"Why are they called Perseids?" I ask.

"Because they seem to radiate from the constellation Perseus."

"Who was Perseus?"

"Perseus was the son of Zeus. He killed Cetus, a monster that was harassing Andromeda, the daughter of Cassiopeia. All the characters in the legend are constellations. Perseus isn't up yet, but he'll be rising."

Terry and I wait. Our eyes are adapted to the dark, and we preserve their heightened light-gathering capacity by using, when we must, a flashlight with red cellophane over its lens. Our dilated pupils do not constrict in the ruby glow.

Straight overhead, the Milky Way splits into parallel streams like stripes down a skunk's back. Meteors flick over singly, in pairs, in bunches spread over several seconds. Some I see out of the corner of an eye. Others seem to head straight toward us before fizzling. A few are so faint I wonder if I have seen them at all.

"This is one heck of a shower," I say. "A four-star shower."

Terry chuckles. "Well, it's a perfect night. I bet we can see two thousand stars. That's about the best you'll do in the Northeast. If we were in Philly or anyplace else with a lot of light, we'd be lucky to see five hundred. And we wouldn't see nearly as many Perseids."

Terry shows me a faint star in the east. I pick it out finally by looking a little to one side. My binoculars show the star to be an extended oval, a glowing ball of lint against the sky.

"That's M31, the spiral galaxy in Andromeda," Terry says. "Farthest thing you can see with the naked eye."

"How far?"

"About two million light years. You're seeing it as it was two million years ago."

"And a galaxy . . .?"

"A galaxy is a big cloud of stars. The Milky Way is a galaxy, almost a twin to M31."

I lower the binoculars and contemplate the smudge of stars. When I ask my intellect to register the time and space of such matters, it balks. A Perseid interrupts. Its wake, scratching the atmosphere a dozen miles above our heads, is now completely fathomable.

As night proceeds, the constellations appear to shift westward—an illusion of motion, like that of the sun, caused by the earth's rotation. Terry points out a K-shaped cluster of about fifteen stars that has risen over the trees to the east.

"That's Perseus," he says. "Perseus the constellation is supposed to look like Perseus the warrior, but I think it looks more like a shopping cart."

I look at Perseus and see wheels, a basket, and a handle.

Perseids continue to punch through the sky, their rate slightly increased after midnight. Other meteors fly at angles to the shower. Terry calls these non-Perseids "sporadics" and says they average ten per hour during summer. Sporadics tend to be brighter than Perseids, because they are more substantial—rocks, instead of dirty flecks of ice.

Suddenly a shriek rises from the edge of the field. The cry sustains itself, wavers, dies in a low gurgle.

"What was that?" Terry whispers.

"A rabbit." I remember one my dog caught years ago. "A fox got him. Or an owl."

Memory of the cry fades in the ratcheting of cicadas and the trilling of crickets.

"When I was a kid," Terry says, "I thought this sound was the wheel of the constellations turning."

The sound triggers memories for me, too. As a child I played with my friends during the long summer evenings, and three things I remember: the ceaseless insect chorus; the acrid smell of lightning bugs (it stayed on your hand long after you released a captive); and the bright fields of stars. I realize I have not taken the time to really look at the stars for years.

"I've always watched the stars," Terry says. "When I was a kid I studied the star maps for months, until one night all the constellations clicked into place.

"When I was twelve, I built a telescope. My mirror looked like a glass pie plate that hadn't been hollowed out. It took me a year to grind it. Then I went down to Buttorf's plumbing and heating shop in Jersey Shore and had them roll a tube out of galvanized steel. For the housing I used pipe fittings—couple of tees, couple of nipples, couple of flanges."

"What did you look at first?"

"The great nebula in Orion. It's a giant cloud of purple gas in the Hunter's belt, where stars are being born. My telescope was a good one; I could pick up divisions in Saturn's rings and the red spot on Jupiter. I could watch the shadows of Jupiter's moons move across the planet."

Terry lowers the back of his chair two notches so that he looks straight up. Meteors bolt past, a long one heading south, two short dazzlers right out of the radiant.

"You know," Terry says, "meteors are kind of sneaky, the way they show themselves for just a second. For years I was convinced one would hit me. Lying out in the fields, I always felt like I was in a shooting gallery. Sometimes I'd have to go inside."

A minute later a long, white meteor splits the sky and explodes in brilliant silence. We gasp.

"That was no snowball. That was a *rock!*" Terry says.

A score of lesser sky travelers pass before Terry speaks again.

"Man, I still love the Perseids. When I was a kid I always counted them during the shower peak and sent my totals to 'Sky and Telescope'—that's a magazine for amateur astronomers. When I was fourteen they published my report, and I felt I was registered with the world."

"Why didn't you become an astronomer?"

Terry folds his hands behind his head. "When I graduated from high school, I went to Cornell on a scholarship to study astronomy. There were plenty of people up there who were a lot smarter than I was. After my freshman year I came back to Pine Creek and lived with my grandfather.

"But I kept up on astronomy, and I still get 'Sky and Telescope.' Maybe just looking at the stars is better than studying them."

Terry takes the binoculars and trains them on the sky. He watches for a moment, then hands the glasses back.

"Look up at the Milky Way. See that black patch in the Northern Cross?"

The binoculars resolve the milkiness of our galaxy into a thousand points of light. I find the Northern Cross and the black patch. In the patch there is nothing.

"That's the Coalsack," Terry says. "It's a cloud of dust spread against the Milky Way, blocking out the stars behind.

"When I was about sixteen, I was watching the Perseids one night when my father came home from prayer meeting. He turned on the porch light, came outside, and showed me a religious tract that said there were parts of the sky that had no stars. It said the scientists couldn't explain it; only God knew why. I was just a kid, but *I* knew what the holes were. I told him about the dust. He looked doubtful, and asked how the astronomers could know that. I was speechless. To satisfy him I would have had to first tell him everything I knew about physics, chemistry, and half a dozen other sciences. I suddenly saw the gulf between us. 'They just know,' I said.''

It is past two o'clock when we fold our chairs. All around, asters spangle the field and the heads of Queen Anne's lace glow like nebulae. We look at the sky and wait until one last Perseid streaks by.

We load the chairs in the car and drive back to town. Traffic lights blink. Beer signs glare from tavern windows. In an all-night diner, people sit under yellow light, eating.

Arteries

Down on the county line on a fine March day I saw a fencerow dying. Skeletal trees, hickories and oaks, lay on the ground pointing
east, the way the wind had made them lean in life. A bulldozer la-
bored at one end of the row, shoving fieldstone into a trench.
Smoke from burning brushpiles smudged the sky.

The next time I passed that way, an unbroken field stretched toward the mountain. The expanse was monotonous and sterile,
with only a skim of snow on cornstubble. Gone were the trees.
Gone were the rocks. Gone were the birds and mammals and the
plant life that had flourished in the fencerow. Gone was much of
the spirit of the land—something that transcended efficiency, pro-
ductivity, and the convenience of plowing a mile-long furrow.

I grew up on the edge of farmland stitched with a healthy network of fencerows. I saw my first fox along one. I encountered the
innocent violence of insect predation in the unruly weeds and
shrubs. I experienced the intensity of a summer thunderstorm,
squatting beneath a fencerow cherry tree that offered precious little shelter. And I received, in a fencerow, hints of an omnipresent
life force straining, never resting, at the seams of human activity—a view of nature that has colored my perception ever since.

A fencerow is man-made, or at least man-initiated. It begins when
a farmer drives posts—often of long-lasting locust wood—to hem
in livestock, create a field, or mark a boundary. He staples barbed

or woven wire to the posts and goes on about his business.

Birds perch on the posts and wire; their droppings release undigested seeds of poison ivy, blackberry, poke. The seeds germinate and take root in the soil. Borne by the wind, seeds of milkweed and dandelion snag on blackberry canes or come to rest in the lee of fenceposts. A passing raccoon pauses to strip burrs and begger ticks from its fur. Over the years, sheltered from the plow, the hitchhiking plants prosper.

Chipmunks and red squirrels find homes under rocks that plowmen pile on the line. The rodents leave walnuts, hickory nuts, and acorns, which sprout into the climax of the fencerow's evolution, trees that grow wide and tall in the open-field sunlight. When they die, they rarely go to waste: Just last week the neighbor was out with his wagon, culling old elm from his lines for next February's firewood.

By far the greatest users of fencerows and their provender are wild things. Animals travel in or near the rows; they hide and build nests in the thick and thorny cover; they feed on the wide variety of grasses, fruits, and seeds, or on creatures attracted by the vegetation.

In otherwise bare land, a fencerow is a travel artery. Pheasants skulk through the long grass. Woodchucks and skunks waddle within a few yards of the protecting hedges. Squirrels journey the lines from woodlots to fields in search of corn; if the fence is a stake-and-rider affair, they commute on the rails. Foxes follow fencerows—if a pair, one takes one side and its mate the other—as much to shield themselves from human eyes as to prey on fellow travelers.

In May and June, the fencerow rings with song: thrashers, robins, kingbirds, song and field sparrows, cardinals, cuckoos, chats. Quail nest in the thick grass, which will arch over a nest and conceal it. Catbirds and indigo buntings weave cups in rose bushes and hawthorns. Flickers, bluebirds, chickadees, starlings, and screech owls compete for cavities in fenceposts and trees.

Rabbits, which could not survive in the limited cover of open cropland, spend their lives in and along the edges of fencerows. White-footed mice, meadow mice, and voles form part of a huge base of short-lived prey animals that reach peak populations in the fencerow's abundance and relative security. Among larger mammals, the woodchuck may be the most important from an ecological standpoint. Many fencerows are honeycombed with woodchuck burrows. Once abandoned, the burrows become dens for skunks, opossums, rabbits, and raccoons. Pheasants use them as temporary hiding places. Foxes kill woodchucks and usurp their dens for nurseries. (The only fox-woodchuck confrontation I ever witnessed ended with a bloodied but determined rodent holding the fox at bay while backing into a fencerow rose thicket.)

The weasel, a slender brown mustelid with a racing metabolism, may be the ultimate land predator in foxless fencerows. Rat snakes lie flat-bellied on rocks, reptilian hearts idling, waiting for mice. Hawks and owls perch in snags, scanning fencerows and the surrounding fields for prey ranging in size from moths to house cats.

Less obvious is the constant killing and consuming and reproducing among insects. Gleaming green tiger beetles subdue weevils. Angular ambush bugs seize bees. Robber flies, long legs folded beneath their bodies, fall upon leafhoppers and ladybugs. Mantises mate—and the female may devour the head and neck of the male as they couple.

The soil beneath the fencerow teems with life—bacteria, protozoa, and amoebas. I once read that 250 pounds of bacteria and an equal weight of microscopic animals and fungi may inhabit an acre of soil. A single gram—one twenty-eighth of an ounce—can support ten thousand lives.

Fencerow plants host slugs, mites, aphids, beetles, grasshoppers, and spiders. To the fencerow come wrens, toads, turtles, snakes, owls. All interact—all participate in the strange and spiraling ascent of life. The farmer who traps his fencerows and kills the wandering fox sets himself at the top of the gyre.

A summer fencerow throbs with a current of life far greater and more diverse than the fields it separates. The huge oaks raise twigs by the thousands to the sky, swaying in afternoon winds. Some of the giants attract lightning and end up smoking and shaking, sawed-off or bearing curved pink fissures the length of their trunks. A white oak down in Slaybaugh Valley took a bolt, and I have watched it for five years. So far it survives, and sometimes on a drizzly fall day I shoot a fox squirrel from its acorn-laden crown.

Autumn frosts begin to clean out the fencerows. The leaves of sumac go blood-red, hang on for a while, and fall. Insects wither to husks, sliding back in their life cycles to the dormancy of eggs. Buck deer thrash the yellowing sassafras; whether they rub remnant velvet from their antlers or battle imaginary rivals, no one can say.

In winter the fencerow is a magnet. Crows share branches in windblown trees. Opossums scour the ground for shriveled grapes. Songbirds shelter in cedars. Always the predators are there, and always the prey. Beneath the fencerow the woodchuck's heart beats four times to the minute.

With spring thaw, the fencerow is a filter slowing the flow of water. In England and parts of Europe, where fencerows have stood for centuries, a field on one side of a hedge may be several feet higher than its neighbor. The fencerow controls erosion and lets the soil in each field seek its own level.

I, too, seek my level along a fencerow.

Sometimes a walk is almost a labor, so intricate and in need of investigation is a fencerow. I poke along, peering into fencepost cracks, overturning stones, sticking my head in bushes. Never mind that catbirds scold and chipmunks pop into burrows and turtles hiss and duck their heads. I am absorbed, and that is enough.

I traveled a fencerow near home not long ago. Past a rusting rake I came upon another of the farmer's castoffs, a broken wood box. As I touched one corner, a rabbit shot from beneath, bounded down the line, and disappeared, slick as any magician's trick.

I kept walking. A kingbird swooped and snatched an insect from the air, perhaps a honeybee out foraging from a colony in a hollow oak. Hundreds of bees were visiting asters, as unmindful of the fencerow's diversity as I was engrossed by it. Had a war been raging—cannon pounding, rifles cracking—they doubtless would have continued to work.

I discovered a pile of fox droppings on a rock (they contained insect parts, and seeds that looked like blackberry); fresh woodpecker work on a cherry tree; and half of a sea-green eggshell, its white inner surface wet. I came upon two dead calves, their legs tied together with baler twine; black-and-white coats and mummy heads, ears chewed to nubs by some scavenger. Maybe I should have taken it as a portent, but I screwed up my nose and went on.

I was pleased with my skills of observation when I spotted a toad squatting in the grass. I watched for a long moment, mesmerized by the minute expansion and contraction of its breathing. On its olive back, brown warts glistened; it sat stolid as a jade buddha.

Even when I knelt, the toad remained frozen. I had picked up a stick and was preparing to prod it into action when I noticed it had no hindquarters. Or rather that its hindquarters were firmly in the mouth of a snake.

A hog-nosed snake. With upturned, pointed snout and black-barred back. Its head, stretched to accommodate the toad, was broader than its body.

Neither snake nor toad budged. I wondered if they were keeping still out of concern for the two-legged predator looming above, or if they were resting after a long struggle, or if—and this frightened and awed me—the snake had no conception it was going to kill, the toad no inkling it would die.

I wanted a test. I wanted nature to send a cricket scuttling by. I wanted to see if the toad, in the jaws of death, might nevertheless seize the cricket.

But no cricket happened past.

In time, the snake worked more of the toad into its mouth. The toad blinked. It stared ahead, pushed at the snake's mouth with a foreleg, and was still.

I withdrew. I stood beneath the bright sun, my eyes focused on a distant fencerow. Beyond stood another, and another, and a fourth riding a knoll on the horizon. How many unheralded births? How many unrecognized deaths?

Insect buzz and tick and trill melded with dry sparrow song. I retraced my path along the fence, trudging home through the rank summer grass, wondering at what I had seen. I realized that not once had I considered freeing the toad.

The Way a Mind Wended

In blue noon light, the tracks are distinct. They were made early this morning after the snow stopped. Since entering the woods an hour ago, I have seen the spoor of grouse, squirrel, and deer. And now this—fox.

The old beagle sticks her nose in a track, flops her ears, and looks up quizzically; snow flecks her gray muzzle. I lift the bolt of the .22 rifle, look at the brassy glint of a cartridge I knew was there.

I curl back the flaps on my hat, exposing my ears.

The tracks are round, regular, and in a neat line. Their size tells me they were made by a red fox, with its large, well-furred paws, rather than a gray. Fur between the pads equips the red for winter, for making a living in the snow, for evading a hunter.

The tracks move off through the oaks; the dog and I follow. For half an hour we tread through woodlots, brush fields, cropland. The new snow covers ice formed when rain and a hard freeze followed an earlier snowfall; the footing is treacherous, and several times I slip, once banging my elbow hard on the ice. According to the tracks, the fox is quite able to negotiate the ice, even to find food on it: At the edge of a field I discover a dot of blood and a few gray hairs where a rodent died. I find where the fox investigated a squirrel's excavations, and where it hopped onto a fallen tree to look around. A snatch of Thoreau pops into my head: "I know which way a mind wended this morning."

I am not surprised when the tracks turn toward a place I had intended to check all along. It is a sinkhole, a landform common in this valley of decayed, subterranean limestone; I saw foxes in the sink in August, when their coats were yellow-red and they looked thin as whippets under the sparse pelage.

I edge toward the sink, rifle ready. From the center of the depression rise jagged rocks, like bad teeth, and a dirt ridge topped by a single pine. My eyes search for a red coat on the ridge, and in the aspens on the other side.

No movement, save the rock of trees in wind. No sound but wind. I have come quietly, into wind.

The tracks slant down the side of the sink. The ice on this sun-facing slope is rotten, and my boots crunch through. The dog follows. At the bottom, I find what I was afraid I might: an oblong depression in the snow with fresh tracks running away. I have ruined my chance at ambush. The fox is gone from its bed, and now we must play by its rules. The dog sniffs the bed, wags her tail, whimpers. She has never trailed foxes, but the fresh scent tells her we will hunt.

The tracks are far apart where the fox bounded up the slope on the far side of the sink. I try to climb, but slide back. I unload the gun and try again, making unsteady progress from tree to tree. The trees run out with ten steep feet of ice left to ascend, and when I try to make it my boots slip. I land on my side, swinging around to slide feet first, fending off trees, skidding to a stop back at the bottom. I try again, and again slide back. I solve the problem by pounding footholds with my heels, then toeing the holds. The old beagle follows in my steps.

Reading the tracks, I find where the fox crouched in weed stubble and watched. The tracks lope away through a grove of pines. The dog follows for a few feet, then turns to see if I am coming.

I wonder if this fox is one that I watched this summer. A nearby den held five pups who wrestled in the alfalfa. They mauled their mother, trying to nurse, until she snapped and warned them away. When they wandered too far, the vixen came to carry them back.

One time she saw me. She charged toward my hiding place and veered aside, showing me the blonde length of her body as she ran barking across the field. The act was effective: When I turned back to the den, the pups had disappeared.

The old beagle puts her nose in a track, wags her tail, whines. I reload and follow her.

We go through the pines, across an old road, and into a decrepit orchard. I find where the fox, on three legs, urinated high on a shock of grass. A dog, then.

I hold some advantages: it is mating season, and my fox may become careless or may attract a companion less wary; I know the lay of the land in these reverting fields and pine plantations; and there are hours before the sun goes down. The fox holds these cards: his senses are more acute than mine; he can run on the snow crust, which I noisily break through time and again; the rising wind may erase his trail; and he must simply elude, not kill.

I fall and slide down a short slope, dragging the gun through the snow. I dust myself off, blow snow from the sight, unload, and clear the barrel with a weed stem. I move on. The trail follows an old railroad grade. Below and to my left, two deer are bedded; the doe's breath jets before her face, and her blunt-nosed yearling dozes, its head falling forward and then jerking back up, like a child trying to stay awake in church. Although the fox did not disturb them, the deer rise when I pass. They bound away, strong and sleek; they are wintering well.

Again I find where the fox stopped to watch his backtrail, his tail sweeping the snow where he sat. Beyond, his prints are grouped in fours, hind tracks ahead of fore. They run for open fields.

I wonder if I will lose him in the fields. I break into a trot to stay hard behind him before wind obliterates all sign of his passage. When I leave the trees, I face a blast of wind. Ice in the corn stubble reflects the sky. Across the valley a red-roofed farmhouse sits at the foot of a mountain; smoke curls from the chimney; the mountain is a series of blue knolls like knuckles on a fist.

Halfway into the field, the fox's tracks are fuzzy, then gone. I look west. Snow rides the wind, smoking on the ice. Beside me the old beagle crouches, ears flying parallel to the ground.

Where would you go if you were a hunted fox? Halfway across the field is a rock pile overgrown with sumac. I nod, blinking in the wind. When I reach the rocks, I find a depression in the snow on the protected side. Faint tracks lead away. I curse my stupidity. I had a chance to come at him from behind a rise, and him bedded down to boot. I threw it away.

He is taking me seriously now; the trail swings wide, through a brushy hollow that bisects the field, then up along a fencerow. On the fence's windward side there is no snow for tracking, but I do not worry: His intent is apparent. He is going back to the woods.

The tracks are restored where fencerow meets trees. Oaks creak in the wind. The dog forges ahead, nose in the trail. We hunt through the overgrown orchard, crossing sign that we—the fox, the dog, and I—laid down two hours earlier. On this sweep through the reverting fields, my fox is joined by another. When I read this in the snow, I stop. The dog jumps up, paws on my legs. Together we wait a cold half-hour, letting the fox forget, I hope, about the man on his trail.

When I start again, I concentrate less on the trail itself than on the cover ahead. The slower pace is comfortable; I am weary high in my thighs and hips, and my knees are sore from falls on the ice. When fox tracks mingle with those of deer, I hold the dog back to keep from confusing the trail further.

In low, still places, fox musk hangs in the air. It smells like skunk but is less pungent and more agreeable. The two sets of tracks run side by side. I know the second fox is a vixen when I find a large spot of urine in the center of the trail.

I begin taking small chances: Twice I cut corners and loop ahead where the terrain tells me the foxes will change direction. Both times I guess correctly but am late and only find marks in the snow. Again the foxes go to the fields, and again I decipher the trail over ice and blowing snow.

34

As we hunt back to the woods, a hawk takes off from the trees. It is slate above, pale gray below; it dodges branches, flying with short, powerful wingbeats. A goshawk, a boreal accipiter driven south by the winter. I wonder that the land can hold enough prey for the foxes and the goshawk, the weasel whose trail I crossed, the owls I have heard here so often.

I follow the trails into a bramble thicket. Here they separate, one doubling back toward the fields, the other heading into a narrow gully that runs south. I do not like my chances in the fields; I know, on the other hand, where the gully ends, and think I may catch my fox there.

I turn and jog off. Five minutes later I reach the spot where the gully levels out into low hills. I stand, pulse racing, eyes watching, listening to my own hard breath. Nothing. No tracks. Snow and ice and twisted trees and a late sky, blue and deepening.

I am shivering. The old beagle sits in the snow. The fox never comes.

In the gully I find a few deer tracks, but no sign of a fox; maybe it sensed a trap. I head back for the fields and home, ready to concede defeat. But one last possibility remains: the sink, where hours ago I drove the dog fox from his bed.

The way to the sink is crisscrossed with deer trails. Dead pokeweed juts from the snow, and red dogwood bristles. At the mouth of the depression, I stop. I smell fox musk. One of the foxes is somewhere in the sink.

Matters have been taken out of my hands, events set in motion. I choose the left side of the low ridge dividing the sink and stalk into the breeze. I move by inches. Under the pines, the snow is fluffy and silent.

At least to me.

But the fox hears and is out of its bed, across an open patch, and behind pines—vanishing noiselessly as I raise the rifle.

The dog never notices, and I must check to be sure.

Tracks. Far apart, rimmed by snow, fifty feet from the marks that set the hunt in motion hours ago.

A dove, pink and gray, hurtles over on its way to roost. The dog and I climb out of the sink, traverse the woods, and enter the fields. Gone is the beat of fox tracks in the snow.

We fight the wind down a fencerow where trees stand above swirling flakes. In the hedge lie gray and tan stones. I pick one up. Limestone, twice the size of a brick, with straight edges. It fits the crook of my arm.

Carrying the stone, I bend back to the wind. I am building a wall, and this stone, this day, will go in it.

My Old Man

Everyone should have an old man. I've got one; he's in his eighties, and he lives on a ranch on a wide, sage-studded plain surrounded by mountains.

How about your old man?

Maybe he stokes a morning fire in a gray clapboard house along the Chesapeake. Down there the land meets the ocean in furtive, tide-washed coves, where strings of pintails and gadwalls and teal explode from the ditch grass, their bellies dripping with sparkling, sun-catching water.

Or maybe your old man has a place up in Michigan. A small house, only a five-minute walk from grouse cover, and six dog pens out back. Five of the pens are empty; in the sixth is an old setter bitch who gets to sleep inside on the coldest nights—they come more and more often these days—and who still gets fire in her eyes when your old man puts on his gun vest.

Or maybe Kansas. Green and wide and cut with brushy ravines. Maybe your old man was born there and has always lived there, except when he was overseas that time so many years ago (the last war humanity would ever have to fight, they said); maybe your old man lives in a white house under cottonwoods beside a slow, ox-bowing creek. Where meadowlarks go up like quail all along the wagon road, and where quail go up like nobody's business when he motions you in on that staunch young pointer he's been working.

Or maybe he lives upstate. On the Pike. Where autumn mountains are red and brown, steep and rugged, cloaked with morning fog. Where deer eat windfall apples under a tree in the back yard (you daren't shoot these deer, or even joke about it), and where you get up in the dark, hear the old man coughing in the kitchen, go out and see the pink wash in the east, walk with your old man as far as his stand, and go on up the mountain to yours.

Maybe your old man has eyes pale as denim that's been washed a hundred times. Or brown, sharp eyes sunk in a thicket of wrinkles. Maybe his hands are spotted and rough like buttonwood bark, his face weathered like a walnut hull that has lain all winter beneath the tree. Just below the cuffs, his wrists may be brown as elk antlers after the bulls have rubbed them against pine. Rain, wind, snow, sun, blurring, ticking heat, quiet cold: All robbed his skin of youth, beat it to toughness, browned and chafed and cracked it.

Maybe your old man wears Western boots, with a special, hand-made pair for shopping for livestock or going into town for the mail. Or arctics, with at least one broken buckle. Or leather-top rubbers bought from the same mail-order outfit year after year. Or birdshooter's specials, with laces knotted where they've busted. Or patched, re-patched, and finally electrician-taped waders.

Hat? Usually. Stetson: rippled, salt creeping from the band, grimy where thumb and forefinger tug the brim toward the eyes. Canvas duck cap: tan or camouflage, faded and shapeless but guaranteed to keep off spray and hide the face from incomers. Wool cap: black-and-red-checked Richie, visor broken, threads raveling at the back, crazy little black button gone off the top.

What does he shoot—if he still shoots? A Model 12 with an action that clatters like a sack of clams? A 35 Rem with a spiral magazine and a kick that'll set you down if you aren't ready? A 30-30 carbine with a triple circle of wire replacing the saddle loop? A Damascus steel double ("English, I don't know the make, that's wore off; it was Dad's; we cut the stock down to fit me, and somewhere along the way Uncle Jack put on a recoil pad and took

38

a couple inches off the barrels, which was a shame, cause that took off the little pearl they had up front for a sight; I think it's out in the garage somewhere; want to see it?'')?

The old man will show you the pearl.

He'll show you many things. Like how to skin a squirrel quickly and efficiently and not get fur on the meat. Or how to lace your boots so they won't keep coming undone and slowing you down in woodcock cover. Or where to hunt turkeys during the last hours of a late-season day. Or where the elk lay up when the wind changes and snow begins to whip out of the east.

He'll show you all these, plus many things less practical and more important. He may even show you yourself in thirty or forty or fifty years.

You're lucky if you have an old man. You're doubly lucky if the old man still has the agility and desire to hunt. And you're lucky beyond estimation if your old man is your father or grandfather.

I have an old man—no blood relation, but as fine an old man as one could hope for. I write to him every month or so, and wish I lived closer so I could drop by and see him more often.

My old man lives in Wyoming, on a ranch he bought about fifteen years ago, before he became my old man. Before that, he and his wife worked a homestead high in the Sunlight Basin of the Absaroka Mountains. But winters are long up in Sunlight—snow flies in October and the melt doesn't come until late May—and they were getting old even then, so they bought the place down on the plain. My old man's wife is gone now. He still ranches a little, with the help of a couple of friends and the day-to-day ease of habit. I met him through my aunt and uncle, who owned a neighboring ranch. Their place had bad water—alkaline, no good to drink—and every few days I would throw a half-dozen plastic bleach containers in the back of the car, drive over to the old man's place, and fill them from his well.

I can close my eyes and see the kitchen. Slick tablecloth, checkered dish towel draped over salt and pepper shakers, sourdough crock on the counter, stockman's calendar on the wall, denim jacket hung over a chair back, crumpled tan Stetson on the seat, mud-flecked boots under it. Half an inch of dead flies in the well of a storm window, and out that window the bulk of Heart Mountain—sere or snow-dusted, dawn-rosy or gray as lead when the days shut down.

I have, over the last five years, spent a fair share of time in that kitchen. My old man tells me that "the latch string is out," which means I may come any time and stay as long as I want.

After meals, my old man washes the dishes carefully—refusing my offer to perform this chore—and stacks them in a metal rack. Often the radio is on, soft but distinct, with "news of Cody and the Bighorn Basin."

My old man sits back down, and we talk. We talk about things we don't like, and things we do, and my old man has plenty of both. He dislikes snowmobiles, the Forest Service (passionately), Charolais cattle, magpies, people who drive across his land and cut his fences, Franklin Delano Roosevelt, and the whole idea of Coca-Cola. He likes a far greater number of things, including Chevrolet pickup trucks, Pendleton shirts, cats, jackrabbits, Hereford cattle, horses (he remembers some he owned forty years ago and still grieves for them at times), people who show spirit and dignity under difficult conditions, Indians, neighbors, and certain memories.

Most of the memories have to do with hunting.

Like the time a bunch of hunters straggled into his cabin up in Sunlight, half-frozen after getting caught in a blizzard. They told him they'd lost a 30-30 saddle gun on the summit of the conical, nameless mountain that towers up on the edge of his homestead, and that he could have the rifle if he wanted to fetch it. He found it the following spring and used it over the decades to take a tremendous number and variety of game.

There was the bighorn killed right at timberline after a long stalk: the sheep all belting past through the talus, my old man's rifle swinging on the biggest, the heavy sound of the bullet striking, the spasmodic kicking of the dead ram.

The moose he woke up to find browsing alder shoots fifty yards from the cabin: the bead front sight silver against the moose's black side, the shot waking my old man's wife, the moose running a few steps toward the springhouse before falling.

The elk: so many he's lost count. Elk taken for their racks, elk bugled in for friends, crippled elk finished off for hunters he was guiding. Depression elk—hillside salmon, government beef—one way to stay solvent when times were hard.

A grizzly taken in the day's last light in a high-country meadow: the first shot breaking the animal's jaw, its outraged bellow echoing from mountains and banks of shadowy pines, the second shot anchoring the bear, the third shot finishing it.

Or the time my old man was guiding, and they spooked a very ordinary mule deer buck out of a blowdown. They already had camp meat and a full packload, but the client wanted the deer, which stood on the edge of the trees watching them. The hunter asked for my old man's 30-30; was reluctantly given the gun; worked a shell into the chamber; and, in so doing, sandwiched the sling between lever and stock, preventing the action from locking. The hunter squeezed the trigger. Nothing. He yanked it. My old man waited until the buck faded into the timber. Then he took the rifle back, saying, "You just have to pull right hard."

My old man talks about hunting and game and the way things were then and the way they are now, and I listen.

I sit across the table from him. The dawn lights his face, or the warm evening light filters into the room from where the sun is setting behind Elkhorn Peak up in Sunlight. My old man talks, and I listen, even though I've heard the stories before. If he knows he repeats himself, I hope he also knows I want to hear.

The Vulgar Bird

In 1890 and 1891, Eugene Scheifflin released 120 European starlings in New York City's Central Park. Scheifflin belonged to the Acclimitization Society, a group dedicated to stocking the New World with exotic species. His personal goal was to give Americans all the birds mentioned by Shakespeare.

Scheifflin's starlings prospered, nesting in hollow trees in the park and under the eaves of the American Museum of Natural History on Central Park West. By 1898, they had spread east to Connecticut and west to New Jersey. They colonized Philadelphia in 1908, Boston in 1914, and Washington in 1916. A cry went up for control, but too late. By 1926 starlings had infested half the continent, and twenty years later they reached the Pacific. In 1979 they nested in Fairbanks, Alaska.

The starling swept across America because it found an ecological niche unoccupied by a native bird—an incongruous, twentieth-century niche that included superhighways, bridge beams, building ledges, garbage dumps, grain fields, hog troughs, and the back yards of split-level homes.

The starling, *Sturnus vulgaris*, probably evolved on the short-grass steppes of Asia. It inhabits the Old World from the British Isles east to Lake Baikal (in the U.S.S.R. north of Mongolia), and it has been introduced in Australia, South Africa, and New Zealand, as well as in North America. It is not a handsome bird. Its black feathers reflect blue and purple and green, like motor oil in a puddle. Its long bill is shaped like a pair of needlenose pliers. Its tail is stubby, its wings triangular, its body chunky. In flight, it looks like a cigar with wings.

Starlings are superb fliers—they've been clocked at forty-five miles an hour, faster than most other birds of comparable size. Often they fly in a band of twenty or thirty, the whole flock making rapid shifts in direction and inclination, as if each member were responding to the same set of impulses. The flocks have a neat defense against an airborne predator: When a hawk or a falcon dives toward them, the starlings bunch into a tight formation that offers no single target to attack.

In spring, the groups disband and individuals begin looking for places to nest. Males spend considerable time poking their heads into dark cavities. They prefer hollow tree trunks and limbs, but will settle for holes in walls, drainpipes, church cupolas, cliff crevices, mailboxes, the burrows of bank swallows, and rabbit holes. A male who has found a likely spot will perch nearby, calling out in a high-pitched squeal and windmilling his wings at passing starlings, trying to lure in a mate.

Because starlings do not migrate in autumn (although they may shift south a few hundred miles in some regions), they are on the spot in springtime to stake out nest sites before cavity-nesting migratory species return. Should migrants find or hollow out a space of their own, starlings are apt to evict them, eggs and all. Flickers and other woodpeckers get pestered out. So do martins and bluebirds. The bluebird population has shrunk drastically in the last fifty years, a decline many birdwatchers blame on the starling.

Starlings seem not to mind apartment living. Since a pair defends only their nest hole and a nearby perch, a half-dozen pairs—each raising four to six offspring—can occupy the same tree. If another bird lands on the family perch, the owner sidles toward the trespasser, forcing it off.

To feed themselves and their young, starlings fan out across the country. They catch grasshoppers, stinkbugs, and beetles. They thrust their bills into the soil to capture grubs and worms. Few birds care to eat gypsy moth and tent caterpillars; starlings have learned to avoid the irritating hairs covering these insects' bodies by scrubbing the caterpillars against the pavement, or by squeezing out the soft inner tissues with their bills. Starlings eat cherries, grapes, olives, mulberries, raspberries, apples, and the seeds of many plants. From perches on grazing cattle they spot insects in the grass. They ride the backs of hogs and leap down for grain when the animals nose open their feed bins. They eat greasy french fry wrappers, animals crushed on the road, and putty from freshly glazed windows.

Starlings shun tall weeds and heavily forested areas, preferring to forage in short grass. They are especially attracted to the suburbs, where lawnmowers have opened up thousands of acres rich in seeds, insects, and worms. The superhighways conveying people back and forth to the cities have further enlarged the starling's food base with mile upon mile of close-cropped median strips and grassy shoulders.

As the starlings in an area prosper, they feel the pressure of their own numbers and expand into fresh territory following a pattern first described in the 1940s by Brina Kessel, a graduate student at Cornell. According to Kessel, it is the first- and second-year juveniles who move: Not yet tied to nesting sites, they are drawn into new areas by grain harvests and ripening fruit. (Today, Kessel is an ornithologist at the University of Alaska. It was she who reported the ultimate result of flock spreading in North America: the 1979 nesting of starlings in Fairbanks.)

In many small towns and city neighborhoods, summer evenings are filled with the metallic, clattering cries of starlings. The birds roost in parks and along streets, hundreds and sometimes thousands to a tree. Their droppings make sidewalks slippery and force housewives to bring in the wash. When people get fed up, they try to persuade the starlings to move, using recordings of the bird's own distress cry, noisemakers, firehoses, and guns. If starlings leave, they rarely go far—into the next block, or across town. Often they are back the following evening.

While summer roosts can be a nuisance, winter roosts are worse. In late fall, starlings join with native birds—grackles, cowbirds, and blackbirds—into large bands that subsist on grain lost by harvesting machines, fresh sprouts of winter wheat, wild fruits still on the vine, and anything else they can scavenge. Fifteen years ago, starlings wintering near Colorado feedlots ate, during the course of the season, eighty-four dollars worth of cattle rations per thousand birds. Considering the size of many flocks, the losses to farmers must be staggering. In 1975, the U.S. Fish and Wildlife Service estimated that 77 million of these birds were inhabiting 71 Louisiana roosts, including 21 million in a single copse of trees. Arkansas had 51.5 million in 33 roosts, Tennessee and Kentucky, 77 million. While most of the truly huge roosts are in the South, states as far north as Pennsylvania also support large wintering flocks, which tend to gather in the same spots year after year.

Scientists studying a California roost found that starlings dispersed up to fifty miles a day to feed. At dawn, following a swelling vocal chorus, the birds lifted up in a great cloud, waves of them flying out in different directions. The scientists estimated that the 2 million starlings foraged that winter over eight thousand square miles, with the average bird traveling farther, over the course of the season, than many transcontinental migrants.

One reason that starlings band together in winter is to keep warm. The big flocks have a knack for finding sheltered places —groves of conifers whose needles break the wind, sloping spots where cold air cannot pool. When scientists in Israel checked temperatures of vacant roosts, they found them ten to fifteen degrees warmer than surrounding areas.

Roosting birds huddle together—studies in North Carolina revealed a mean of 56 and a maximum of 195 starlings per square meter. In 1965, an ornithologist showed that four starlings roosting together in air temperatures in the mid to upper thirties cut their metabolic rates in half compared to starlings roosting alone. When food was withheld from the grouped birds, they survived three days of cold weather. Loners lasted one day.

Some observers believe that individual starlings occupy the same perch in the roost night after night. If so, says an Israeli scientist, it pays to perch high. He stacked starlings in wire cages one above the other, so that droppings from birds above fell on those below. After three weeks, he sprayed his captives with water to simulate a cold rain. The lower their roosting spots, the more water the birds absorbed; wet birds lost heat more quickly than dry birds did, used more energy keeping warm, and died at a higher rate. The scientist reasoned that acid from the droppings had broken down oils waterproofing the birds' plumage.

The ground beneath a large roost may be several feet deep in droppings, dead birds, and broken branches. In a North Carolina roost, 2.3 million birds deposited an estimated 3.75 tons (dry weight) of droppings nightly. In Kentucky and Tennessee, many people say the guano is dangerous. They argue that it fertilizes the ground, spurring growth of a fungus, *Histoplasma capsulatum*, whose windborne spores cause a human respiratory disease, histoplasmosis, endemic to the region. The disease is usually mild, like a cold or the flu. Although many people get histoplasmosis, science has never linked it conclusively to bird roosts. But people believe the birds responsible, and in years when the roosts seem especially crowded, they clamor for action.

In the winter of 1975-1976, responding to a particularly rabid outcry, the governor of Tennessee ordered a roost in a state park sprayed with the insecticide Fenthion. National Guard helicopters delivered the chemical, normally used for mosquito control, at a reputed dosage of eight pounds per acre—one hundred times the rate permitted by the Environmental Protection Agency. Fenthion killed a few starlings and blackbirds, along with some cardinals, sparrows, blue jays, hawks, and owls.

A more effective weapon—and one that leaves no lingering toxic residue—is a detergent, Tergitol. Sprayed during rainy, chill nights, Tergitol mimics the effects of bird droppings on plumage: It washes away protective oils and causes the birds to die of exposure. When it works, Tergitol kills by the millions. Other chemicals have been touted as possible weapons, including a poison called Starlicide, and several sterilizing agents. The Fish and Wildlife Service is supposed to be developing a potent contact poison, but it won't be released for several years, if then. Some observers believe a large-scale siege against winter roosts might actually benefit the starling, whose ability to adapt and to reproduce quickly could boost its numbers at the expense of blackbird and grackle populations.

While the big rural roosts grab the headlines, other starlings spend quiet winters in the cities. In New York, they roost in the Times Square billboards, soaking up heat from thousands of light bulbs. They perch on roofs near chimneys. They enjoy dry, snow-free perches on the horizontal steel I-beams holding up bridge decks, and on the intricacies of Victorian buildings. Generally they ignore devices intended to shoo them away: searchlight beams, sticky chemicals that burn their feet, sharp metal spikes, stuffed owls. Their droppings stain buildings, damage car finishes, and offend people. Flocks must sometimes be cleared from runways before airplanes can take off or land. In 1960, a turboprop Electra crashed at Boston's Logan airport, killing sixty-two passengers. Chopped-up starlings were found in the plane's engines.

Generally, city dwellers have adjusted to starlings as they have to smog, noise, and other urban inconveniences. On rare occasions, though, they have fought back. In Waterbury, Connecticut, police officers trained shotguns on a flock and killed two thousand starlings with a single fusillade. A chemist at Syracuse University, Benjamin Burtt, built large chicken-wire traps on roofs of downtown buildings. Baited by grain and decoy birds, starlings landed on perches and slipped into the cages through tight, funnel-like openings. Once inside, they could not get out again—there were no perches near the holes, and with their wings outspread and fluttering, the birds could not squeeze through the openings. In the winter of 1964-1965, the traps captured 55,000 starlings, which were gassed and disposed of.

Not surprisingly, starlings are mistrustful of man. You

cannot walk up to one and brain it with a rock, as you might a robin. To explore this wariness, I decided to run an unscientific experiment. One March morning, a dozen or so starlings were perched in the bare branches of a walnut tree behind my house. I got my .22, went into the bathroom, and lifted the window. The birds sat preening and wiping their bills against the branches at their feet. I took aim and squeezed the trigger.

At the gun's report, one starling fell and the rest departed in a flurry of wings. I reloaded. The birds flew in a big circle and landed in the tree again. I aimed, shot, and killed a second bird. All of the rest took off for parts unknown.

The next day, they were back. I went into the bathroom and eased up the sash. The birds flew. Later, I saw them in the tree again. I went out a door on the opposite side of the house, rested my rifle on the corner wall, and shot. When I tried that maneuver a second time, the starlings flew just as I got my gun in position. The time after, before I made it to the corner—apparently they'd heard the door opening.

After that, the only way I could get a shot was to sneak out while a truck was rumbling past on the highway, tiptoe to the corner, kneel, and ease my rifle around.

It didn't seem worth the trouble.

Hiking on Your Stomach

In the Rocky Mountains a few years ago, we met a man on the trail. He was dressed in hiking shorts, an unbuttoned flannel shirt, and heavy leather climbing boots; a red bandanna held his sun-bleached hair out of his eyes. He was traveling with his dog, a rangy German shepherd. He ordered the dog to lie down and it did, growling softly.

The man's name was Roy. He professed to be a photographer on assignment to shoot pictures of elk. His face and arms were deep brown, his legs and torso hard with muscle. He squinted away across the rolling, grassy mesa and asked if we'd seen any elk.

We'd seen a few down at timberline. Roy told us he spent every spring, summer, and fall making photographic forays into the mountains—the Uintas, the San Juans, the Salmon River Range. He liked to hike for two or three weeks and then come down to a town where he could get a shower, mail in his film, and replenish his food supply. Food, for Roy, was both energy and calendar. When he set out on a trip he would pack several loaves of bread, a jar of mayonnaise, and cans of tuna fish, one can for each day on the trail. He subsisted entirely on tuna fish sandwiches. When the cans were gone, his trip was up.

My hiking partners and I looked at each other. Roy gazed at the jagged, circling peaks, speaking softly.

It had been his experience that a man can live quite adequately on tuna fish. Still, he gets hungry—sometimes almost irresistibly

49

hungry—for other kinds of food. Roy believed he could bankroll many future expeditions by peddling food to other backpackers. His plan: Get a donkey. Build a sturdy box, with dozens of drawers and shelves, and lash it to a packsaddle on the animal's back. Fill the box with the exotics to which the mind, hungry and deprived, inevitably turns. Apple pie. Cherry pie. Fresh eggs. Oranges. Banana cream pie. Chocolate layer cake. Mark the food up several thousand percent, head off into the wilderness, and seek out hungry hikers. Carry no granola, no freeze-dried beef stroganoff, no powdered Tang. Not even tuna fish, although, God knows, a man can live on it. Fresh raspberry pie. Angel food cake. *Cheesecake.* Saliva showed in the corners of Roy's mouth.

We left him sitting among the alpine flowers; I suppose he went back to his camp and had a sandwich. We hiked a few more miles, pitched the tents, and cooked dinner. I don't remember exactly what we had; perhaps mashed potatoes laced with cheese, or bulgar with dried vegetables, or lentils with onions and bacon, followed by pudding or fruit for dessert. One night we had trout almondine: the fish, stocky and deep of draft, duped on grasshoppers and yanked from a rushing creek, cleaned immediately, dusted with bread crumbs, and laid in the frying pan; the rice sprinkled with chipped almonds and annointed with soy sauce.

On that trip I was traveling with Joe Ebaugh, and I always eat well when he is around. We had hot cereal and pancakes on many mornings, and twice Joe retrieved from the depths of his monstrous blue backpack—we had dubbed it The Blue Hotel—an aluminum Dutch oven in which he baked, in the coals of our fire, the most delectable coffee cake I have ever eaten.

Not infrequently I found myself looking over my shoulder to see if Roy and his shepherd were creeping up on our camp.

Joe, and his brother Phil, have a formula for determining how much food to carry into the woods: two pounds per person per day. For three people on a two-week trip, that's eighty-four pounds. I have actually gained weight on Ebaugh trips, despite having to stagger along beneath a pack that towered into the sky, loaded with all my equipment plus my share of rice and spices and noodles and tea and cheddar cheese and Ralston and cocoa and liquid margarine and dried peaches and cocoanut and split peas and peanut butter.

I always gripe at the weight, but I would rather carry too much food—even carry some of it out of the woods on the last day—than go hungry, as I did on my first big backpacking trip. Three of us had decided to tackle the remote Wind River Range in west-central Wyoming. We read in some book that your pack should weigh no more than one-third of your body weight, and we kept religiously to this limit. We left out camp moccasins, extra underwear, camera tripod, binoculars. We pared our food list after deciding that we could catch fish for a few meals. And we took to heart the messages printed on the crinkly foil packages of freeze-dried food: "Six servings." "Package serves four." "Enough for three adults."

Enough, we decided later, for three adult female midgets leading sedentary lives at sea level.

As our beards thickened, our cheeks grew hollow. We flogged the streams and lakes but failed to catch a fish. All traces of pudginess disappeared from under our belts, and the skin tightened across our ribs. We nearly fell to blows when one of our number spilled a pot of freshly cooked butterscotch pudding. (I can still see it seeping into the pine needles.) Sitting around the campfire, stomachs rumbling, we would speak not of the day's hike or the sky full of brilliant stars; not even of women; but of prime rib and steamed shrimp and what we might do to a grizzly bear unlucky enough to blunder into camp.

Adding to our misery was the freeze-dried food. The portions were not only meager, they tasted bad. One especially vile dinner—we'd bought several packets of it on sale—was turkey tetrazzini. It tasted like sawdust into which a little chicken bouillon had been drizzled. Turkey Tet Offensive, we called it, but we ate it and wished for more.

About the only food we had in abundance was "gorp." The

term is backpacker slang for any mix of dry foods—nuts, candy, fruit—meant to be munched while hiking. Ours was not an especially imaginative blend: M&Ms, peanuts, raisins. Almost immediately we divided our communal bag into three shares. As our hunger deepened, gorp became our currency. One might offer to do the dishes, out of one's turn, for a quarter-cup of gorp. Cooking the turkey Tet Offensive *and* cleaning up afterwards was worth at least half a cup. Each man guarded his gorp, portioning it out day by day, hour by hour; it became a contest to see whose supply would last the longest. The irony was that none of us especially liked gorp, and our capacity to stomach it eroded steadily. To this day the thought of that combination—M&Ms, peanuts, raisins—almost makes me gag.

In theory, gorp alone can supply all the basic metabolic needs, at least over a short period. Many people have thriven on less. Ben Lilly, a renowned lion hunter in the Southwest, is said to have mixed honey and peanut butter in a jug; following his hounds on the trail, he would spoon out the food as needed. Old Finis Mitchell, who probably spent more time wandering in the Wind River Range than any other man, said, "You don't have to eat as you would at home. My wife makes a fruitcake that has everything in it that the body needs. But it gets tiresome eating fruitcake three times a day, so we have a sackful of materials for breakfast and combine them most any way we want. We mix Grape Nuts, Gerber baby oats, baby rice, and wheat germ. Now they've got that new stuff, granola, and I throw a little of that in. Then I add powdered cream and sugar. All you do is put it in a plastic pan and mix in water."

They say an army marches on its stomach. The axiom applies equally to backpackers and to back-country hunters. Often when backpacking, you feel no great need to hurry. It is part of the experience to rise and travel at leisure, taking time to enjoy the unspoiled terrain. It is permissible to let the sun warm your tent before you climb out of the bag; you may dawdle over breakfast, cooking a meal that not only fuels your body but also lifts your spirits, making you better able to appreciate the surroundings.

A hunter is set to a higher pitch. He is out to enjoy nature and landscape, but he is also on a mission. Slow, elaborate meals are generally out. If someone in the group wants to hunt close to camp, quit early, and cook supper for those who wander in later, he is applauded. (He can be disagreeable, impolite, even obnoxious, but he is likely to be the first person invited on future trips.) Breakfast, though, is another matter. Who wants to get up in the dark to cook a fancy meal? What's needed is something quick, warm, and filling: food that will let you reach your chosen ridge before dawn, while freeing your mind to think like an elk or a deer.

Bob Bell, editor of the *Pennsylvania Game News*, has arrived at such a breakfast. It is fast, it dirties a single pan, and it stays with you, perhaps a bit heavily, until lunch. It consists of four courses. First, a cup of instant coffee. While drinking the coffee, you fry an egg. The egg is eaten between two pieces of bread (toasting, optional). The cup, drained of coffee, is filled with fruit cocktail, a product, Bell reports, that provides more fruit and less syrup than any other canned fruit. Since you gulp your cocktail straight from the cup, there's no need to dirty a spoon. (Presumably, you are allowed to chew.) Next, a refill of coffee. This cleans the cup, leaving only the frying pan to scour with a little sand. "You don't have to fiddle around for an hour and a half," Bell says. "Can get right to hunting."

Bell also has devised a method of telling when your trip has gone on too long. It relies on a can of vienna sausages, those slippery, tubular links encased in gelatin. "When you start thinking about opening that can," he says, "you know it's time to get off the mountain."

Sooner or later, almost everyone does get off the mountain. You may be gaunt, or just honed nicely and still in possession of several pounds of rations. It either case, you will make a beeline for an eatery. If you're lucky, you'll choose a fine restaurant and they'll let you in. The Irma Hotel in Cody, for instance, where you can order a thick T-bone broiled to perfection; or, perhaps out of spite, a trout dinner. Maybe you'll end up in an out-of-the-way adobe, with enchiladas and tortillas and real Mexican beer. Even a quonset hut-turned-hamburger palace, from whose depths a fresh-faced waitress will appear with a fixed smile (Who *are* these hairy hillbillies?) and a tray, loaded with gut bombs and french fries, to hook on the lip of your car window.

When we got out of the Winds after that first bumbling trip, our clothing baggy and our food sack flat, we drove wild-eyed for the nearest dot on the map: Cora, Wyoming. We barged into the town's only building, a white-painted store with a false front. A microwave oven, something of a rarity in those days, stood on the counter below a plastic sign depicting to unrealistic advantage a selection of burgers and hot sandwiches.

Giving our orders to a gray-haired woman, we swept through the aisles, each of us returning with a heavy bag of cookies. The microwave sat there, ticking. We leaned against the counter, waiting. The proprietress smiled. "Backpackers?" she said.

FROM THE KITCHEN OF JOE EBAUGH:

Sailor Joe's Rip-Off Buns

plenty of margarine	cinnamon
handful raisins	good deal of honey
handful brown sugar	biscuit mix
handful walnuts	

Following Bisquick directions, make double batch of biscuit mix. Grease Dutch oven with margarine. Spread half of biscuit mix on bottom of pan. Add half-a-handful each of raisins, brown sugar, and walnuts. Sprinkle with cinnamon. Dot liberally with margarine, drip with honey. Add the top layer of biscuit mix and cover with remaining raisins, brown sugar, and walnuts. Bake until done. "Times are iffy," Joe says. "It depends on how hot your coals are. Set the oven on a good, heavy layer of coals. Mound some coals on top, and up there build a series of two or three small stick fires. You're more apt to burn the bottom, so keep the top hot—that's doing most of the baking—and cook for as short a time as possible."

The Showing is Nightly

The showing is nightly.

It runs over in Slaybaugh Valley (not the valley's real name; for selfish reasons I don't want the show sold out, not even for one night), and it starts at eight, give or take an hour.

Rough clothes are de rigueur: boots, brown canvas-duck pants, a green chamois shirt—tan will do if your green is in the wash—and over the shirt a mesh camouflage parka, preferably with hood. I also bring binoculars (good ones, as I like to watch the actors closely) and a bottle of Cutter's to keep the bugs away. Ample parking can be had down by the old iron furnace or under the maples standing guard at the cemetery.

When I arrive, I ease the truck door shut and drift toward the woodlot. I don't scuff my feet, I don't slap gnats, I don't cough.

Last Tuesday the first act began as I walked along the edge of the cornfield. A woodchuck was feeding in the alfalfa beyond the tall, green-waving stalks. I squeezed inside the first row of corn, which ran parallel to the tractor road. By walking while the woodchuck fed and keeping still when it looked around, I was able to get a fine seat—so close I didn't even have to use the binoculars.

This woodchuck's specialty was pantomime. First he gave his impression of a bear: He shuffled, he shook his head, he looked quizzically about, he snorted a bit. Next he moved onto the tractor road, sniffing and weaving in fair imitation of an overfed, underworked hound. Then he got up on his hind legs, balancing

55

nicely by using his belly as a counterweight, and gave a fine impression of a rotund, self-satisfied little man—a banker or an undertaker. I whistled sharply by way of applause, and he was gone behind a curtain of grass.

Half an hour passed before the second act got underway. By then, I'd settled into the best seat in the house, a rounded, foot-deep ditch screened on both sides by high foxtails. To my left was an alfalfa field, to my right the stubble of harvested wheat. I waited for the actors patiently, entertained by monarch butterflies riding the evening breeze and a red-tailed hawk that flapped out of the woodlot, towered to a speck on the face of the sky, and drifted east.

The sky was a flawless blue. If this night turned out like the previous two, the breeze would vanish by dark. A heavy dew would coat the land and cold air would slip like molasses into low spots. Night before, there'd been a frost in the Barrens, a few miles north of Slaybaugh Valley, according to a man who is working there. He said it was light, a ''water frost'' that did no damage to vegetation, but a frost nonetheless. This is the third week in August.

I looked out in the stubble field. There, burnished in the slanting sun, was a fox: As usual, the act had begun before I'd even been aware of it.

I focused the binoculars. The fox was all angles—sculpted ribs, pointed nose, tapering shanks. Her eyes glittered. Her paws and legs were black, as if she'd walked through a burned-over field. She trotted diligently through the stubble, ears directed forward, and now and then she would stop, cock her head, and sniff. Finally, she tensed and jumped. At the top of her leap her body curved like a trout over water, and when she came down her front feet lit on a pile of stalks that the harvesters had left. Catlike, she darted left and right and came up with a vole in her mouth. She dropped it, pawed it, picked it up again, slung it into the air.

She left the rodent where it fell and went back to patrolling. A few minutes later, she killed again. This time she took her prey to the woodlot, reappeared a few minutes later, picked up the first

vole, and made off with that one, too. I thought it too late in the
year for her to be feeding pups, so perhaps she was caching her
take—burying it, then marking the spot with urine. I found myself wondering why; in August food is everywhere, and lean times
are still far off. Perhaps she'd felt the frost, too.

Her act had three more scenes, each a variation on the first, each
acrobatic and full of drama. She made her last kill after a series of
side-to-side leaps, a moment of waiting—body tense, tail twitching—and a pirouetting, slashing pounce. She shook the vole and
let it fall; then she cocked her ears, lifted her head, and looked at
the sky. A second later, I heard it, too: the muffled wingbeats of a
flight of birds. It sounded like applause.

While watching the fox, I'd become aware of the deer—had
glimpsed them filtering onstage, emerging from the woodlot and
fading in and out of the corn. Now I turned my binoculars toward
them.

About a hundred yards away stood a doe and two fawns. The
doe was looking in my direction—perhaps she'd seen me turn.
The sun was behind me, though, shining in her eyes and making
further staring useless and probably uncomfortable. With a shake
of her tail she went back to feeding. The fawns were carbon copies
of each other, still long-legged and blunt-nosed, their rusty coats
marked with pale spots that would vanish when their winter pelts
came in. They fed calmly, then kicked up their heels and bounced
through the grass like gazelles across a veldt.

Something fluttered over my head, banked, and planed off my
field of vision. As it swept back, I saw it was a barn swallow. It had
a long forked tail, sharp-elbowed tapered wings, and an orange
belly.

The swallow circled tightly, mouth agape as it swept through
clouds of insects. Through the binoculars I saw the insects fleet-
ingly, as one sees muscae volitantes, those curled, transparent
spots that float on the surface of the eye; and out beyond the insects, over the alfalfa, the fencerow, and the oats field on the next
farm, scores of swallows twisting in flight.

The crowns of the woodlot oaks had begun to flame a green-tinted orange. Behind me, the sun was setting. The sky was pale on the horizon, shading to a deep blue overhead. Down the valley the ridge was sharp, the trees distinct as the warp of a rug. The sun rested on top of the mountain, outlining ridgetop trees and spreading its last glow. Averting my vision, I could detect its downward crawl.

Impatient, cheating myself of the sunset, I rolled back onto my belly.

More deer had joined the herd; an even dozen ranged over the field, some lying in the grass, others standing, tail-wagging and cud-chewing. They were lazy and careless. It was not yet time to rut, or to fear men, or to search seriously for food. Centerstage, a pair of bucks casually shook heads at one another. Both had narrow, forked racks, in velvet. They feinted, but never actually touched antlers. One closed in and began to lick the neck and muzzle of the other.

Movement drew my attention to the edge of the field. A spike buck slipped out of the woods. Behind him came a second buck, this one with more of a rack, then a third, and—at the rear of the entourage—a deer with antlers wide and tall and swollen with velvet. The year before, a fine eight-point had run Slaybaugh Valley; I had hunted him unsuccessfully, hadn't heard of anyone taking him, and felt sure that this was the same deer. The shape of the antlers was similar—main beams curving out from the brow points, then angling up sharply—but this year his rack branched into ten points. He stood on the fringe of the herd, ears working like radar dishes.

The light was beginning to fail, and fireflies signaled over the alfalfa. The rest of the deer fed around me, but the big buck hung back. As I watched, details began to go: His rack dissolved, the outline of his back faded, and finally I couldn't tell when his head was up or down.

I lowered the binoculars.

The show was over, at least for me. Crickets shrilled, and down by the pond a bullfrog gave its vibrating call. I could have stayed and listened for owls or waited for a moon to throw light on the scene, but I'd had my fill.

I rose to a crouch, sneaked back down the furrow, and gained the shelter of the corn without disturbing the deer. Walking quickly, I descended into a hollow lined with cold air. Then I was out of the corn and on my way up the final hill, my boots thumping the wagon road.

Behind me, in front of me, around me, I knew the show was going on. Going on in all its splendor, its intricacy, its mindless self-perpetuation. All of which no longer suggested a play, but a circus—a three-ring circus inside a three-ring circus, ad infinitum.

It was there, going on, and it would always be going on. It would be there when I started the truck. When I got home. When I went to bed. When I woke in the night and closed the window against the chill. Characters, whole casts would be out there playing in earnest, playing, fading, relinquishing the stage.

The showing is nightly.

The Decoy

There exists a beauty of utility, a patina laid down by use and age. It's a silent and confident beauty, different—you can't really call it better—than the raw, salty beauty of newness or birth.

Think of a duck decoy, cracked and bleached by sun, wind, and waves. Shot holes stipple one side, and the ballast is worn smooth.

Think of a black dog, a retriever. Its muzzle is gray, its eyes clouded. Patches of fur are worn away where hips and shoulders rub the floor when it lies down.

Think of a man. His scalp, pink through close-cut hair, is marred with pale scars. The weather has reddened his hands, neck, and face. The face is open, its features rough.

The decoy, I own; the dog and the man live in my imagination.

I bought the decoy, a redhead, from an old woodcarver whose shop stood on the sandy edge of the road running down North Carolina's Outer Banks. The carver sat on a stool, his knife making the final cuts on a shorebird—it looked to be a dunlin or a knot. He told me the decoy had been made around 1900 by a man named Levi Perry. Levi—he pronounced it "levee"—hailed from Kitty Hawk and hunted the bays, sounds, and saltwater inlets sheltered by the barrier islands of the Outer Banks. The old man told me to smell the base of the decoy. I caught a whiff of sea air and the clean scent of cedar.

These days, the redhead sits on a shelf by my fireplace. As decoys go, it's no work of art. Four rusty spikes hold the head to the body, and the paint, or what's left of it, looks as if it were slapped on in a hurry. Still, there are concessions to form: The head has a neat taper, the bill is complete with hooked tip, and old Levi clearly caught the jaunty, head-back conformation of a redhead.

At the turn of the century, a decoy didn't have to be perfect. The Outer Banks were wintering grounds for tremendous flocks of ducks and geese, perhaps the greatest concentrations the world has ever seen, and all that was necessary was to set out a battery of ten score decoys, crouch in the floating, coffin-shaped box, and wait.

When I rub my hand over the decoy, its patina takes me back seventy-five years. Back to a short, sinewy man named Levi Perry; a barrel-chested Labrador retriever; gray clouds boiling out of Albemarle Sound; and the vast, glistening reaches of bay and marsh and ocean and sky, dotted with waterfowl.

Was Perry a market hunter? Likely—most able-bodied Bankers were back then, and the simple utility of his decoy, plus its hard use, point in that direction.

I imagine him poling to his battery before dawn, a breeze off the mainland bringing scents of brackish water and tidal plain soil. The Lab would be quivering, ears cocked, eyes searching the gloom. I picture Perry at first light, looking out on the great rafts of canvasbacks and goldeneyes and scaup that have drifted, in the night, around his battery.

Does he hear the quiet talking of ducks across the water, the rumble of batteries opening up down the length of the Sound? Does he shoot as the sun climbs out of the Atlantic? Does he dip the barrel of his shotgun in the water to cool it? Does he stop to watch the wheeling redheads, the ragged vees of geese, and the swift-flying buffleheads, and does the sound of their calling fill him with humility and wonder that he, a man, has been set down at this time, in this place?

And does he pick up his battered pump gun and shoot again—because it is the only thing he knows to do?

I don't know. But it's all there. It's written on the decoy.

Sulfur in the Air

In the fifteen seconds it takes you to read this paragraph, lightning will jab the earth fifteen hundred times. Most of the strokes will spend themselves harmlessly. Others will shatter trees, start fires, and stop the hearts of beasts and men. Somewhere, somebody will see the flashes. They will scare him, or make him curious. They will fill him with awe.

The Micmac Indians believed thunder was the sound of seven rattlesnakes whipping their tails as they flew across the sky. The Delawares decided the heavenly violence came from spirits of the rain, fighting to protect the Indians from evil forces. To the ancient Greeks, lightning was a weapon Zeus slung at his enemies. Aristotle didn't buy the supernatural explanation; lightning, he said, was a burning wind unleashed by the collision of a "dry exhalation" with a cloud.

Today we know that lightning is atmospheric electricity. Ben Franklin proved it in 1752, by flying a kite in a thunderstorm and draining off some of the current, which behaved in exactly the same manner as the electricity produced by a hand-cracked generator.

A lightning bolt is a channel of electricity an inch or two across, two hundred feet to twenty miles long. Its temperature is 50,000 degrees F, four times as hot as the skin of the sun. Hitting a tree, lightning sets the sap boiling—so fast that the trunk explodes. It can gouge a ten-foot crater in the ground, split a boulder in half.

At 90,000 miles per second, it races from the earth up to the belly of a cloud—and not in the other direction, as our eyes tell us. Its passage expands the air in a massive pressure wave that reaches our ears as thunder.

Each year, thunder sounds a knell for some two hundred Americans—golfers, campers, rock climbers, horseback riders, hunters, fishermen, farmers, boaters, baseball players. Lightning kills more people than any other weather catastrophe, including tornadoes, hurricanes, blizzards, and floods. Four of five victims are male, presumably because men spend more time outdoors than women. Stay-at-homes also share in the attrition: One-quarter of all victims get blasted indoors.

A stroke of lightning can deliver up to 125 million volts—ten thousand times the current of the electric chair. A jolt sears the skin. Sometimes it sets the hair on fire, and often it blows off one shoe as it exits the body. Lightning kills by short-circuiting the body's electrical system, shutting down heart and lungs. Still, "deaths" are often reversible; if a victim's heartbeat and breathing can be reestablished, he may recover completely.

Lightning doesn't always kill or injure. Sometimes it just plays tricks. It has wrenched scissors from the hands of seamstresses, twisted the tines of a farmer's pitchfork, stripped the clothing off young girls, melted jewelry, singed beards, clobbered livingroom lamps, and made clock hands whirl backwards. Lightning sealed a soldier in his sleeping bag by melting the zipper. One bolt blasted a desk, catapulting a typewriter into the ceiling with such force that it stuck.

Some people get hit more than once. Although the odds are heavily against receiving a second strike (let alone surviving it), a fellow named Roy C. Sullivan—"Dooms" Sullivan, a retired park ranger living in Waynesboro, Virginia—has been clipped by lightning seven times. Sullivan bears scars on his right arm and leg from a bolt that decked him in 1942, while he was leaving a firetower. He was hit again in 1969 (eyebrows singed); 1970 (left shoulder burned); 1972 (hair set on fire); 1973 (knocked out of his truck, hat and hair ignited, left shoe ripped off, and underwear scorched); and 1976. Sullivan was fishing in 1977 when he attracted his seventh bolt. It burned his chest and stomach, landing him in the hospital for four days. "You can tell when it's going to strike," he says, "but it's too late. You can smell sulfur in the air, and then your hair will stand up on end, and then it's going to get you. You don't have time to do anything."

Lightning usually picks off its human victims by ones and twos, but it often wipes out livestock by the bunch. During storms, sheep and cattle huddle together, and a lightning charge will pass instantly from body to body. Even a near miss can kill a large quadruped, whose four legs span more ground than do a human's and thus pick up a greater shock.

Lightning starts three-quarters of the forest fires in the United States, each year burning more than $30 million worth of marketable timber. It destroys $20 million of other property, and is the top cause of power outages.

Lightning can flicker through a snowstorm or a sandstorm. It can dart among the clouds of ash above an erupting volcano, along the edges of a nuclear fireball, and even from a cloudless sky—the proverbial bolt out of the blue. Usually, though, it shoots out of a thunderstorm.

Storms come in two main types. Convection thunderstorms develop when sun-warmed air rises high in the sky; frontal thunderstorms occur when a mass of cold air plows under a warm mass. In both cases, the rising warm air is cooled, and the moisture in it condenses into a cloud. The center of a swiftly ascending cloud is a swirling, tumultuous place. Ice particles and water droplets collide, picking up electrical charges. Positive charges float to the top of the cloud, negative charges sift to the bottom. As the cloud marches across the land, its negative base somehow creates a positive charge on the ground. The ground charge follows the cloud, an invisible electric shadow flowing into trees, hills, and steeples, straining to join the negative charge in the cloud. Air, a poor conductor, discourages the tryst.

What happens next is too fast and too faint for the eye to follow. The cloud sends down a "stepped leader," a crinkle of current that steps fifty yards in a millionth of a second, pauses for fifty millionths of a second, and steps again. The path may split several times. Ten, twenty, up to forty steps later, the leader nears a high point on the ground. Behind it, a path of electrified particles stretches back to the cloud.

The moment the stepped leader touches, a return stroke races up the path. The return stroke is the lightning we see, a quicksilver pulse of energy that heats the surrounding air to glowing. Although lightning actually moves from the ground up, we perceive its dazzling zigzag as a heaven-to-earth movement, our eyes deceived by the initial stepped leaders.

As the main return stroke subsides, secondary strokes called dart leaders fork out of the cloud. They bombard the earth three, four, five, up to two dozen times. The dart leaders retrace the main channel, avoiding the stepped leader's dead-end branches that never made it to the ground.

In a stiff wind, the dart leaders may fan out in a luminous band known as ribbon lightning. Sometimes they fall apart in glowing fragments tens of yards long, called chain lightning. No one has ever explained chain lightning, or a third rarity, ball lightning, a grapefruit-sized, glowing orb that rolls about on the ground or bobs through the air, only to disappear with a pop or a bang.

The normal lightning sequence takes about a second. The part we see—the return stroke and the dart leaders—lasts perhaps a fifth of a second. A stroke or a leader lights the sky for several thousandths of a second, and is separated from the next flash by a few hundredths of a second. The eye can barely make out the individual strokes, which is why lightning seems to flicker.

During a thunderstorm, only one lightning strike in five actually links a cloud with the ground. The others flash inside a single cloud, or go from one cloud to another. The "heat lightning" blinking on the horizon on humid summer evenings is usually cloud-to-cloud or intracloud lightning. You hear no thunder from this distant fury because sound waves tend to curve upward in the vicinity of a storm; if you're farther than fifteen miles from a stroke, its rumble will pass right over your head.

It's easy to tell how far away lightning is. Count the seconds between the flash, which you see instantly, and the thunder, which travels about a thousand feet per second. Multiply the number of seconds by a thousand to get the distance to the storm in feet. (Example: Lightning, followed ten seconds later by thunder; ten times one thousand equals ten thousand; ten thousand feet is roughly two miles.)

If lightning strikes within a few hundred yards, you will hear an earsplitting bang the instant you see the flash. Sometimes the bang follows a hissing or clicking noise, which may come from the downward-moving stepped leader, or from land discharges straining to meet the leader.

When lightning gets this close, take precautions. Stay away from tall objects. Resist the impulse to hunker under a tree, as lightning striking the tree could travel through its root system, and kill. If out in the open, don't become a lightning rod: Lie down, in a swale if possible. Metal attracts lightning, so avoid flagpoles, antennas, golf clubs, tools. Never go boating during a storm— you're a prominence out on a lake or a bay. Never swim—lightning can travel two hundred feet through the water.

The best protection is to sit in a car with the windows rolled up, keeping well away from any metal part. You'll be perfectly insulated—not by the car's rubber tires, as many people believe, but by its metal shell, which will usher current into the ground. If indoors, keep clear of electrical appliances, telephones, and light switches.

What are the chances of being hit? About one in a million, depending on where you live. Uganda, the lightning capital of the world, weathers some 240 thunderstorms each year. Florida has 90, Maine 20, California 10. Pennsylvania gets about 40 storms a year.

A more pertinent statistic, contends Martin Uman, a University of Florida scientist who has written several books on lightning, is the number of lightning strokes per square mile per year. These figures have been determined from photographic surveillance, from records of strikes to power lines, and from counting machines activated by lightning-emitted radio waves. According to Uman, the number of flashes hitting one square mile of ground is equal to 0.05 to 0.8 times the thunderstorm days per year. In Pennsylvania, expect between 2 and 32 strikes in the square mile surrounding your home; in the Ugandan shooting gallery, up to 192.

Each day, lightning strikes the planet eight million times, delivering twice the voltage of all the United States' electric generators combined. Unfortunately, there's no practical way of intercepting the bolts. Lightning is too spread out—even in an active thunderstorm region you'd need 100,000 towers, each 1,000 feet tall, to capture the 100 million watts generated by a small power station.

What good, then, is lightning?

Lightning may have been the spark that started life. In the laboratory, scientists have found that powerful electric jolts can reassemble the four gases of the earth's primordial atmosphere—methane, hydrogen, ammonia, and water vapor—into amino acids, basic components of living organisms. As man evolved, lightning must have provided him with fire. Lightning and thunderstorms help maintain the earth's negative charge, necessary for the production of nitrogen, essential to plant growth.

If you are normal, however, you will banish any thoughts of the indispensibility of lightning when you find yourself underneath it.

One day in August, three friends and I carried our packs along the Continental Divide. In the Absarokas, just off the southeast corner of Yellowstone Park, the Divide is a broad, flat mesa. At two miles above sea level, the mesa is treeless. Lichened rocks litter its dusty soil, and lupines flower blue where snowbanks dribble toward pale lakes.

All afternoon, thunderheads had sailed over the high country like a fleet of dreadnoughts. Rain and soft hail spattered our coats.

Lightning flashed, distant strokes whose thunder rumbled off the peaks. That evening, we hiked down off the Divide and tented in a grassy saddle above a wooded ravine. Clouds massed, sealing out the sun; we laid out our pads, fluffed the sleeping bags on top, and crawled in.

I don't remember which of the two wrenched me awake—the incandescent flash or the blast that buffeted the earth. My stomach went liquid, and I tightened in a trembling fetal kink. How close? Fifty feet, a hundred? The ledge above camp? A tree on the saddle?

Rain roared against the tent. Another flash and its simultaneous, ear-cuffing crack. I rolled on my back and lifted my feet and head; perched on the short scrap of foam, I might be insulated. In my mind's eye I saw the metal tent poles beckoning a leader. I plugged my ears and clenched my eyes.

A minute passed. Then, somewhere on the rimrock, the third bolt slammed—not quite as bright or as loud as the first two. When the next stroke hit, there was a distinct lapse between flash and thunder.

Slowly I relaxed. Rain lashed the fly, sagging it. Thunder boomed across the ravine.

Cast Iron, Basic Black

The Pfisters had the most remarkable stove. It was tile, blue-green like the ice tunnel through the Rhone Glacier, and it occupied one whole corner of their kitchen. The cat curled up on a nearby shelf. Dish towels dried on wooden racks. There was a bench where my brother and I could sit with our backs against the warm ceramic.

Frau Pfister gave us coffee that was mostly milk. She sat at the table sewing, or reading, or peeling apples that came from a double row of closely pruned trees. Herr Pfister read the newspaper and told us about avalanches and airplane crashes in the Alps.

He fed the stove. Its firebox did not open into the kitchen, but into an unheated hallway separating the house from the barn. Herr Pfister would push straight pine logs into the stove, where they snapped and snarled until he shut the firebox and closed the damper. On the other side of the wall, the stove poured its steady, even heat into the kitchen.

Although that was twenty years ago, I still remember the hospitable warmth. The memories flood back with special clarity when the fire in my own stove is snapping, filling my house with the same somnolent glow.

I have been heating with wood for seven winters, long enough to obtain some perspective on this activity variously seen as an onerous retrenchment, a step toward self-sufficiency, a renunciation of technology, and a way to reestablish ties with the earth.

Actually, the main reason I burn wood is that no other heat

warms me as fully. Wood heat seems to bake its way into the body, toasting the bones. It's not just psychological, either. Most schemes for keeping warm depend on convection, moving masses of heated air from one place to another. Wood stoves heat by convection, but also by radiation—heat traveling in electromagnetic waves. Just as sunlight leaps through space to warm the earth, heat waves from a stove strike and warm nearby objects. Dogs, for instance, which seem to spend their winters in orbit, extended or close, around hot cast iron. Woodburning an onerous retrenchment? Just ask a beagle.

Soon after I got my stove, I realized that burning wood is an ideal pastime for a writer. Every fire needs a periodic poking to waken smoldering logs, and setting aside pen and paper in favor of a poker has much the same effect on the mind. On the other hand, writing within woodstove range exposes one to the hazard of naps. Let me get a good meal in my belly and find a comfortable spot on the couch, and I'll drowse my way through a whole evening when I'm supposed to be working. If this essay seems full of fits and starts, you'll know why.

Over the last seven years I've discovered that there's a lot more to burning wood than putting kindling in a stove, lighting it, shoving in a log or two, and basking in the warmth. You can, of course, take the easy way out and buy your stovewood. Prices are reasonable, and there's always one woodcutter willing to undersell the next. Or, you can bring in your own wood.

I enjoy woodcutting. I look for the dead trees, the diseased, the tall but crooked ones whose broad crowns intercept sunlight better used by shorter, straighter fellows. By removing the undesirables, I upgrade the quality of the small tract of woods I own. By no means, however, do I take every potential cull. They are too many, and besides, I like some of their shapes. I leave a tree if woodpeckers have been chiseling insects from its bark, or excavating nest chambers in its trunk. I'll spare a big, gnarled oak that drops bushels of acorns for turkeys and deer, or one with a bird's nest in a fork.

70

I like the challenge of directing a tree's fall. I decide where the tree should go, notch the trunk on that side, and saw from the opposite. The tree quivers and leans. If it threatens to fall to one side, I bear the saw in that direction, leaving a hinge of wood on the other side of the kerf to tug the trunk back on course. If the tree hangs up in a neighbor, I use a peavey—a medieval-looking device with a spiked end and a movable metal arm—to wobble it free. Then, the penetrating thud of a tree hitting the ground.

With the tree down, I buck it into stove lengths. Branches touching the ground, or a partially suspended trunk, set up pressures and tensions within the wood; I must pay attention or risk binding the saw.

Wood must be split to get it into burnable chunks, and to allow it to dry; green wood is full of water that a fire must boil off before it can consume the wood itself. Splitting is probably the least popular task among stove owners, and many gravitate toward various mechanical splitters. I prefer a maul (an axe with a fat head), or, for especially tough billets, a heavy sledge and steel wedges.

To split wood, one must read the grain, taking into account cracks and knots, driving the maul to counter the way nature and circumstance bound the tree together. Some woods yield readily: red and chestnut oak, red maple, ash, sassaffas, pine. A white oak's interlacing fibers often put up a good fight. Apple, elm, and beech are even more obstinate. If the gods had really wanted to punish Sisyphus, they'd have handed him a maul and pointed toward a pile of black gum logs.

When my father bought his stove, I thought he should get some practice splitting, so I hauled him a load of mockernut hickory that had been down for a year. All the other hickory I've encountered has split fairly easily, but this batch rebounded the maul with every stroke. I brought some oak and showed Father how easy splitting could be. He agreed, but refused to take up the maul again. It was weeks before I could coax him back to work. His reluctance may have stemmed from shrewdness; as I recall, I split most of his wood that year.

After it is split, wood must be aged. It should be stacked off the ground and out of the weather to dry. I assemble my woodpiles like Herr Pfister did his. At each end of the stack and at strategic points between, I build supporting pillars—four sticks laid parallel to the long dimension of the pile, on top of them four pieces at right angles, then four more parallel, and so on, as high as the stack is tall. I fill in between the pillars, listening to the satisfying *plink* as each stick falls into place. Finally, I take my maul and tap the fronts of protruding sticks so that the pile presents an even face.

A friend who applauds low technology heats his shop with a stove fashioned from a thirty-gallon drum. In the morning, he tosses in corncobs and used motor oil, igniting a furnace-like blaze in a matter of seconds. My fires take more time. A handful of white oak shavings (the gift of a basketmaker) gets the draft moving and fills the room with a clean scent. Sassafras or maple sticks provide a burst of flame. Long-lasting oak or hickory, or sweet-smelling apple, keep the stove piping all day long.

A few statistics reveal the considerable energy imprisoned in wood. One cord of seasoned oak (a cord is a pile four feet high by four feet deep by eight feet long), burned in an efficient stove, yields as much heat as two hundred gallons of oil, eighteen hundred pounds of coal, or sixty-five hundred kilowatts of electricity.

Heating with wood is catching on in a big way. In Pennsylvania, one household in every five heats with wood; another survey estimates that the number of wood stoves in the country jumped from one million in 1974 to five million in 1978. I haven't seen any newer figures, but judging from the stove ads spread through so many magazines, sales remain brisk.

The other evening, sitting by my stove, I read these lines penned by Benjamin Franklin in 1744: "In these northern colonies the inhabitants keep fires to sit by generally seven months of the year; that is, from the beginning of October to the end of April; and, in some winters, near eight months, by taking in parts of September and May.

"Wood, our common fuel, which within these hundred years might be had at every man's door, must now be fetched near one hundred miles to some towns, and makes a very considerable article in the expense of families."

Students of woodburning have wondered if twentieth-century Americans have enough wood to heat their homes without denuding the land. No need to present their calculations; most agree that firewood cutting will not harm our forests. Selective cutting, removing substandard trees and shifting growth to the more economically important individuals, should actually improve the woods.

Still, three years ago it was a far simpler matter to buy a permit, drive onto forested public land, and cut fallen trees within spitting distance of the road. Now a woodcutter may have to haul his fuel a hundred yards, or find a landowner willing to part with trees. More and more people aren't bothering to ask—they're known as "wood pirates" in this district, and they pilfer woodpiles as well. One periodically hears rumors (unsubstantiated) of a quarter-stick of dynamite, secreted in a log, putting a pirate out of business.

In Franklin's day, the colonists burned their logs in open fireplaces—a practice that consumed huge amounts of fuel while squandering most of the heat up the chimney. The Franklin passage prefaced a description of his wood-miserly Pennsylvanian Fire-Place, a forerunner of today's stoves. The invention featured sealed joints and a rear-wall baffle that limited oxygen to the fire, slowing its rate of burning while radiating increased heat to the living quarters. Twentieth-century stoves are even more efficient. Virtually airtight, they can be dampered down to let a fire leak heat all night. A physicist recently estimated that the combination of a modern airtight stove and a chain saw reduces the labor of heating with wood to less than one-twelfth of what it was in the colonial era.

Several friends fell and buck their trees using crosscut saws ("two-person saws," I have been asked to call them). Not a true anti-technologist, I wouldn't dream of mothballing my chain saw, let alone dismantling the shower or carting my refrigerator to the dump. On the other hand, I'm not enamored of the "technological fix," the notion that increasingly complicated mechanical solutions can take care of all our problems. Please keep your five-thousand-dollar heat pump; I'll take mine in cast iron, basic black.

A Fair Day for Hunters

The turkey hunter has spent his day on the mountain. Quiet and still, moving but little, he has seen a grouse leaving roost at dawn, a gray fox hunting, two bucks sparring. In late morning, he spotted two gobblers a hundred steps away, along a stream that covered the small noise of his stalking. The gobblers spied him immediately and vanished on long legs. The lean, dark shapes excited the hunter, but he knew it would be useless to call. Instead, he kept sneaking along, hoping to work into a flock, break it up, and then call in an inexperienced bird. Now, at dusk, he strains to hear wingbeats of turkeys going to roost. If he hears them, he will be back in the gray dawn a scant twelve hours later.

The pheasant hunter returns to his truck. Ten minutes of shooting time remain. His legs are leaden, and walking through the ankle-high grass requires effort. Twice today he wanted to quit—it is late in the season; he encountered no other hunters and half-believes all the birds are gone—but he makes himself continue through the rose tangles and weedfields. Fifty yards from the truck, a farm lane crosses the field. Here, where the grass runs out, he flushes the day's first rooster. The bird flies up big and squawking, and for the pheasant hunter everything slows down, compresses. He sees the iridescent head, the spurred legs, the ring of white feathers around the neck. He swings his shotgun but commits the beginner's error of shooting for the big, gaudy body and not for the head and neck. He hits too far back, in the tail, and the

75

bird never even shudders but flies beyond reach of a second shot, finally touching down, a small speck running to cover in a distant field.

The rabbit hunter is missing a beagle. She and her bracemate provided him with three rabbits (scenting was good on an inch of new snow), and now he finds her tracks mingled with a pheasant's. He knows she chases pheasants silently, and realizes she may be a mile away. He takes off his coat and lays it in the snow. If she comes back, she may stay with it. His shoulders feel the cold. His hands tingle, and his legs are numb under soaked pants cuffs. If he finds the beagle at the end of the trail, he will have to walk back for the coat. But he won't mind. The way he feels now—throat hoarse from calling, stomach knotted at the thought of finding her hit along the road—tells him that the joy of his hunting lies not in shooting game but in cooperating with his headstrong little hounds. The second beagle on a leash and the empty gun crooked over an arm, the rabbit hunter starts to walk.

The duck hunter is cold, too. Water breached a weld in his waders before dawn, when he was setting decoys. Now he squats in the blind and shivers. It has been a good day for ducks, a fair day for hunters. Low clouds smudge the horizon, rain slants, marsh grass nods. All about is the lap of water, a sound that makes any place feel a dozen degrees colder. The duck hunter tries to keep from shivering, and fails. His dog, a big, ripple-coated Lab, sits black and short-eared and business-like in the corner of the blind, tawny eyes watching the sky. The duck hunter glances at his partner. Faded hat. Squinting eyes. Unshaven jaw set below blue lips that suddenly whisper "Sprigs." Whistling wings set off a paroxysm that leaves shots echoing, a pair of pintails floating, a dog swimming, and two men grinning and ready to call it a day.

The grouse hunter sucks a lip whipped fat by an alder shoot. His feet are soaked, he has slipped, banging a hip and scarring his shotgun's stock, and briar scratches quilt his wrists. He is ecstatic: His setter pup has pointed his first game, a grouse the hunter brought down with a whirling, hurried, going-away shot. He reaches in his game pouch and touches the bird's feathers. The pup, run into a state of semi-exhaustion, is quartering nicely, and the hunter resists the urge to call him in and head for home. A wise decision. The pup stops, flanks twitching, head swiveling slowly and locking into place like a heavy door closing. The grouse hunter goes in and does a double take at the woodcock sitting a foot from the dog's nose. The woodcock flushes, the dog lunges for the twittering bird and misses, the hunter starts to shoot, thinks he shouldn't so as not to reinforce the pup's faux pas, decides to shoot anyway, hesitates, and misses. Twice. The grouse hunter looks at the dog. Already the setter has learned one of his sire's tricks: to transfer blame by staring, as if no canine error could compare to a master missing such a small and fluttery thing as a woodcock.

The dove hunter is hot and sunburned and scratching chigger bites on both ankles. His shirt sticks to his back. He has killed seven doves with twelve shots and considers the afternoon an unparalleled success.

The squirrel hunter has walked through frigid woods all day and failed to see a squirrel.

The deer hunter, for the thousandth time this season, pushes his rifle's safety half off and clicks it on again. Since mid-morning, after a bitter watch at dawn, he has scalloped the ridge at a pace of one hundred yards an hour. He stands on the mountain's edge, scanning the bench below. Sleet ticks against the oak leaves. Half an hour passes. He gets ready to backtrack to the ridge spine, go another hundred yards down the mountain, stop, and check the bench again. Then he sees the buck. Or, rather, realizes he has been looking at it for a long time. Sleet dusts the deer's back. Its antlers form a narrow **Y** on each side of its head. Its ears twitch, and the hunter realizes it was just such a movement that gave the deer away. The deer hunter feels his pulse race as it did when he killed his first buck half a lifetime ago. This deer—he braces the rifle against a tree, sights behind the animal's shoulder, and finally eases the safety all the way off—is worth more to him than any trophy rack driven by other hunters. Later, when the forkhorn is hanging in the apple tree, the deer hunter will look at the buck and think of a character in a Faulkner novel who looked at his mule and saw through him, as through a spyglass, the broad land, the sweat, and the desperation of life.

Country Matters

A few years back, I lived in a white cottage with a red metal roof and a broad view of cornfields and a long, blue mountain. The cottage was an expanded and remodeled summer kitchen, where farm wives cooked in summers long past to keep from overheating the adjacent farmhouse; or, it was a collection of small frame structures, including at least one chicken coop, cobbled together to make a dwelling. (I heard both stories. I leaned toward the latter.)

Since I was only renting, I wasn't too keen about tightening up the house, lathing and insulating the floor above the crawl space, adding new window screens, or truing up the thresholds. Thus I found myself sharing space with other tenants.

The spiders were first. Each spring they asked themselves in through gapped floorboards or hatched from eggs secreted behind the stove or under the couch. They wove their webs in the angles between chair seats and legs, in the high corners of rooms, between window sashes and screens. I considered scattering osage oranges when a friend told me that the knobby, green fruits, found in a few local fencerows, exude an odor that puts spiders to flight. But the spiders minded their own business, and they caught the various flies that, in their turn, also entered my home.

I had bluebottles. I had green-sheened speedsters, tiny but perfectly formed houseflies, and big barn flies that droned at the windows trying to get out again. Horseflies would circulate through the house, until I'd trap them in the bathroom and plaster them with a wet towel. Flies flew near my mouth, lit in my food, disturbed my sleep. Even winter provided an incomplete respite: Warm spells drew out squadrons of big, blunt-headed dullards that flew legs-dangling and could be snatched from the air. I once read that the flies of winter should be shown no mercy, to slow the new year's onslaught. I showed none.

Summer, of course, was the busy season. Zebra-legged mosquitos hovered in the shower. Moths sneaked in and flattened themselves on window screens or batted against lampshades. At night the gnats would enter in hordes, fleeing the dark to find death in my spiderwebs and ceiling lamp.

When nights grew long and frosty, a new set of interlopers appeared. Crickets gravitated to my dwelling's warmth, hiding in dark places by day. Sometimes I would lift a shoe or open a closet door and expose one. It would crouch motionless, its antennae rising as if energized, then loose outsize legs and hop under bed or chair.

Mice found a way in (just where I never knew), and at night I often heard them running in the attic. Their musical footfalls descended a scale among the high octaves.

I didn't mind the mice. They were fairly quiet and stayed in the attic away from my food. Red squirrels were a different matter. One chewed its way through the wall by the rain gutter and found some walnuts I was drying in the attic. On more than one crisp blue morning I wakened to the sound of nuts being rolled and gnawed. A better soul might have risen to enjoy the dawn; I pounded the ceiling and cursed. Finally, I caught the culprit silhouetted on the roof—walnut in mouth—and, in long underwear and unlaced boots, toppled him with a .22 shot. To quote an otherwise gentle and tolerant friend, "I am God in my own garden."

At the auction, the crowd filled the yard of a once-white frame house. Behind the house a gray ridge rose into a milky sky. The auctioneer wore a cowboy hat, beard, and vest. He stood on an overturned packing crate while two helpers, an old man and a boy, passed him sale items.

"Sweeper. 'Lectralux, you ladies know this is the best brand, good condition, gotta get twenty for it, who'll give me twenty? Twenty, twenty, twenty dollar bill, twenty, fifteen, fifteen, ten. Ten dollar bill. Ten dollar, ten. Fifteen? Fifteen, fifteen, fifteen. Twenty? Twenty-five? Twenty dollar, twenty dollar, twenty dollar bill. Twenty-two fifty? Twenty, twenty, twenty. Twenty dollars to Mr. Bubb.''

A core of people did most of the bidding, with an occasional nod from the group's edge, where knots of men talked low. Men wearing billed caps with emblems: John Deere, Agway, Peterbilt, Red Fox Chewing Tobacco, Trapper Supply. Women in pastel raincoats and plastic kerchiefs bought crocks, canning jars, and washtubs filled with knickknacks. Men bid on wheelbarrows, tools, a stuffed deer head, a woodstove.

I took the traditional auction stance, hands in pockets. My feet were cold. At familiar faces in the crowd I smiled, careful not to nod.

Listening, I learned that the house was for sale. The seller would take an apartment in town. He was a widower, his children scattered. A drinker. His legs going bad. He would fade in the new surroundings. Just fade away. But then you never could tell.

A bandsaw, gas can, push broom, lunchbox, chest of drawers, bed, table, radio.

When the auctioneer got to the guns, the fringe of the crowd drew in. Men lifted up their faces. The auctioneer paused. His helpers placed the firearms on blankets at his feet.

I glanced at the house and in the doorway saw a figure standing gray behind a screen. It never moved as alien hands hoisted rifles and shotguns. The auctioneer chided the crowd, humored it. The guns sold for good prices. Afterwards, the figure went away from the door.

A friend, a man in his sixties, told me he does not feel accepted by his neighbors, even though he has lived two decades in the same house, raising a family, losing a wife. The problem is that he moved into this rolling, farmed valley as a grown man. He doesn't go to church with the natives. They've never asked him to hunt with them, or to butcher hogs, or make hay. Men who have spent their lives in the valley address him with reserve.

I, too, am an outsider. I was born and raised here in the heart of Pennsylvania, but my family hails from the Midwest, and I grew up in an insular college town some ten miles west of my cottage.

Most of the people hereabouts come from German farming stock. My name is wedged between Fausts and Fetterolfs in the phone book. (Apparently there are even degrees of Germanness: I've heard Amishmen with names like Yoder and Peachey call non-Amish Ishlers, Fultzes, and Schaeffers "the English farmers.") My natural speech is not the native argot, a tongue marked by midsentence inflection rises, transposed word orders (a throwback to the German), and local expressions, although I can and do turn the dialect on if the situation calls for it.

I may be an outsider, but I've developed my own ties to the land. I've traveled its woods, its gentle mountains, its brush patches, and its fencerows. I know the wild plants by sight if not by name, I can sense when the frosts should come and the ice go out of the streams, and I know the kinds of terrain different wild animals favor. I am more at home in the country—this country—than I could ever be in town, including the one where I was raised.

I tried once to live unto myself in the country, but the simplicity did not sustain me. The walks along the fencerows and up Tussey Ridge, the cutting, splitting, and piling of wood, the tinkering with machinery, the foraging, the puttering with bees, the evenings spent sitting on a stump in a woodlot watching deer, the reading and writing—were not enough.

Some thrive on the solitude. I know a woman who spent a winter in a cabin in the nearby Seven Mountains. Snow isolated her for weeks on end; she read, wove a hammock of dyed rope, taught herself to whistle. More often than not, she was more satisfied alone than she would have been with other people. Except at dusk. Then, when the winter sky gave way to night and the woods settled to silence, she felt incredibly lonely, needing someone with whom to share the beauty. The pain would slowly vanish, she said, when she went into her cabin, cooked supper, and turned to her pastimes.

It hurts me too much to be that self-sufficient, and I'm glad. I fear turning my mind in on itself, learning to bear loneliness with no end in sight. But people do it out here. An old woman I know, a farmer's daughter who never married, lives in two rooms of the rambling family homestead, surrounded by souvenirs of four generations. A friend wrote me a letter, saying he was snowbound and without company—"It just keeps coming white as far as you can see."

I know a little about the gathering white, and about houses where the spiders are your friends, and I will say the country is no place to be alone. I suppose it is much the same in town. It's just that country aloneness seems harder to disguise and easier to embrace.

Destroying Angels

The mushroom was white. It stood almost to my eight-year-old knees. A shaft of sunlight penetrating the summer woods lit its cap, the ring of tissue around its stem, and the cup surrounding the stem's base. We were collecting, my father and I. We had found earth tongues and coral fungi and boletes and many other mushrooms, but none so impressive as this white sentinel.

My father was behind me on the trail, so I dug up the mushroom and hurried back. When I gave it to him, he took one look at it and ordered me to wash my hands in a nearby stream. After I obeyed, he explained: I had picked a mushroom so poisonous that particles of it, stuck to my fingers and accidentally swallowed, could have made me deathly ill, and a piece the size of my thumb could have killed me.

He spoke the mushroom's name: Destroying Angel. I remembered the name for many years. When I grew interested in mushrooms again almost two decades later, the Destroying Angel was the first one I studied.

The Destroying Angel is *Amanita virosa*. It belongs to a large and widespread group of fungi, the amanitas, which has been affecting humans for centuries as food, religious symbols, hallucinogens, and poisons. No one really knows how many species of amanitas exist. A respected mycologist recognizes seventy-five worldwide, while the U.S. Department of Agriculture lists over six hundred species, subspecies, and varieties reported from places as various as Perth, Australia, and Blowing Rock, North Carolina.

Like other mushrooms, amanitas are the fruit of underground organisms called fungi; the mushroom corresponds to an apple, the fungus to the tree. Amanitas often push up beneath a real tree, their underground fungal network forming a relationship with the tree's roots. The fungus gets organic food from the roots, and in turn gives the tree minerals.

Amanitas are large, showy mushrooms. Many measure four or five inches across the cap, and they come in a rainbow of colors— red, orange, brown, yellow, gray, green, and, of course, white. Although only a few kinds of amanitas are toxic, they cause over 90 percent of all fatal mushroom poisonings. The Destroying Angel is the most frequent killer in North America; in Europe, the major culprit is the Death Cup, *Amanita phalloides*. Within the last few years, the Death Cup fungus has immigrated to America, probably clinging to the roots of ornamental shrubs. Collectors have found the greenish-capped mushroom in Pennsylvania, Virginia, Delaware, New Jersey, New York, and California.

Unfortunately, many mushroom eaters—"mycophagists," they're called—take to the woods with barely skimmed field guides, blissfully ignorant of Death Cups and Destroying Angels. They look for the mushrooms their grandparents ate in the old country, or they rely on old wives' tales to determine edibility. One bit of folklore says a poisonous mushroom, or toadstool, will tarnish a silver spoon. Another declares a mushroom edible if the skin of its cap peels easily. A third says poisonous mushrooms never grow on rotting wood. A fourth holds that rice cooked with a toxic mushroom will turn red. All of these beliefs are false, and each year people who rely on them are poisoned. Even textbooks give no complete answer: A mushroom's appearance often changes as it matures, and basing an identification on a single photograph can be a costly mistake.

No one knows how many people die from mushroom poisoning each year, but probably scores in America and hundreds in Europe. One of the most tragic incidents occurred in Poland in

1918, when thirty-one children died after eating a mushroom dish at school. In 1975, a Swiss newspaper reported fifty-four local deaths from mushroom poisoning during a short period in late summer. In California in early 1984, several Indochinese refugees were killed after mistaking amanitas for edible mushrooms in their native country.

As part of a general move back to nature, increasing numbers of Americans are eating wild mushrooms, and many are poisoning themselves in the process. Foragers confuse Destroying Angels with meadow mushrooms, the group that gives us our common grocery-store variety. Or young amanitas, called buttons, are picked along with puffballs, which they resemble. (When preparing puffballs, the wise mycophagist slices his specimens vertically; an amanita or other gilled mushroom is revealed by a miniature but perfectly formed stalk and cap.)

People who eat wild mushrooms should learn to recognize amanitas. Even though some are edible, it makes sense to avoid the group entirely. (One should never eat any mushroom unless it can be identified beyond doubt. A cardinal rule: Refrigerate several uncooked specimens of any mushroom eaten. If sickness occurs, a mycologist at a botanical garden or a university can identify the species, and a doctor can start appropriate care.)

An amanita has two distinguishing characteristics. The first is a cup-like structure, called a volva, at the base of the stem. The mushroom looks like it is growing out of this cup. The second characteristic is a white spore print, a pattern laid down by thousands of microscopic spores (the mushroom's reproductive cells, like seeds) falling from the gills on the underside of the mushroom's cap. To check a spore print, separate the cap from the stem, place the cap gills-down on a piece of black paper, and wait two or three hours. If the mushroom is an amanita, a white-on-black, negative image of the gills will appear. Other mushrooms may make pink, light brown, purple-brown, or black spore prints. A few non-amanitas have volvas, and some make white spore prints, but only an amanita exhibits both.

Amanita toxins are potent. A single bite of mushroom can bring on an agonizing, lingering death. The stem, gills, and cap are equally deadly. The toxins survive cooking, freezing, drying. And while most poisonous mushrooms cause symptoms an hour or two after they're eaten, an amanita doesn't tip its hand for six to twenty-four hours. A victim may enjoy another meal, perhaps finishing his collection of wild mushrooms, go to work, even sleep while the poison invades his body.

Finally, he is seized by stomach pains, violent vomiting, and diarrhea. But purging the system does no good, for the mushrooms have already been digested. If the victim is not hospitalized, and if he ate more than one average-size mushroom cap, the illness worsens and usually causes death.

In a hospital, doctors can relieve the vomiting and diarrhea and correct the dangerous dehydration they produce. The patient feels better and seems to recover. He may even be discharged if his illness has not been diagnosed. Then, three to six days later, the symptoms reappear. In more than half of all cases, the victim dies. An autopsy reveals massive liver and kidney damage.

Over the last ten years, scientists have traced the poison's path. The first symptoms—vomiting and diarrhea—start after the toxin enters the bloodstream through lesions it causes in the stomach and intestines. Later, while the victim seems to be getting better, the poison is traveling to the liver. During the second bout of illness, the poison kills individual liver cells. If the patient hangs on, his blood takes the toxin to the kidneys. The kidneys try to excrete the poison with the urine, but it injures the kidney walls and re-enters the blood. It returns to the liver to do more damage. And again to the blood, the kidneys, the liver.

In the past, no antidote existed, although some doctors fed their patients a sugared hash of the stomachs of three rabbits and the brains of seven, based on an incorrect belief that rabbits are immune to amanita toxins. Today a chemical called thioctic acid seems to be saving lives, but it is still considered experimental.

As mentioned earlier, not all amanitas are poisonous. After

87

learning about the group, I decided I had to try one of the safe species to compare its flavor with those of the morel, the shaggy mane, the sulfur polypore, and other wild, edible mushrooms I've learned to identify and enjoy.

I settled on *Amanita vaginata*, the *grisette*, or gray, widely eaten in Europe. A few days later, I found and picked two dozen grisettes on the edge of a golf course. I took them to my father, a mycology professor for thirty years, and he verified my identification. I cooked the amanitas in butter and ate them over toast.

I think my stomach was jumpy even before I lifted a fork; there are no records of poisoning by the grisette, and I knew rationally that I was not eating toxic mushrooms, but I had read too many accounts of slow, sure deaths. I never finished my meal, and for two days after I found myself checking for the dreaded delayed pains. I have not eaten grisettes since.

The most prolific mushroom-eaters are wildlife, and even they steer clear of amanitas. Dr. O. K. Miller, in *Mushrooms of North America*, writes that he has never found rodent tooth marks on a white amanita. ''The rodents have apparently learned their lessons well. They may shy away from the chlorine-like odor which is often very faint to strong.''

Miller's observation points to a possible reason why the Destroying Angel and the Death Cap evolved their toxins: to guard against being eaten, improving their chances of maturing, releasing spores, and reproducing. Many species of plants and animals protect themselves with bad-tasting metabolic products, but why an organism should develop such a deadly, slow-acting poison remains a mystery. Also, toxic power can vary from mushroom to mushroom. One Destroying Angel may have little or no poison, while another a hundred yards down the path may be loaded.

Often we assume that everything in nature—every property, structure, or behavior—must have evolved in response to an environmental pressure. Maybe an amanita's poisons confer no advantages, and it is only plain bad luck that they kill.

To Eat Crow

As the war of 1812 was winding down, an American soldier took advantage of an armistice to go hunting. He crossed the Niagara River into territory occupied by British troops. He saw no game on his hunt except for a crow, which he shot.

A British officer heard the shot. Determined to punish the intruder, he approached just as the Yankee was reloading. The officer, unarmed, complimented the soldier on his shooting skill and his fine rifle, and asked to see the gun. When the soldier handed it over, the officer turned the weapon on its owner and reprimanded him for trespassing. To further humiliate the American, the officer ordered him to take a bite out of the crow. The soldier's pleas fell upon deaf ears, and finally he was forced to obey.

The Britisher warned the American never to cross the river again, handed back the rifle, and wheeled to return to his camp. Now it was the soldier's turn. He bade the officer halt or be shot. Then he ordered the Englishman to finish eating the crow. The officer blustered, begged, and proffered money, but the soldier held firm.

According to scholars of the language, this confrontation 170 years ago launched the phrase "to eat crow"—to be forced to do something repugnant, to abase oneself. English is full of folk sayings like this one, some as old as the Bible and others as young as yesterday.

My grandmother had a favorite—"Nobody will notice on a

galloping horse.'' She quoted this to her children whenever they complained about having to wear this blouse, those socks. I was looking through some books, trying to trace Grandmother's saying, when I discovered the story behind eating crow. I never did locate the galloping horse, but I found a herd of others.

I had always wondered where the term "maverick" came from. It turns out that a Texas rancher in the early nineteenth century, one Samuel Maverick, was lax about his branding. Whenever anybody ran across an unmarked steer, they called it a maverick. The word has since come to mean a loner, a nonconformist, a dissenter.

Returning briefly to the subject of grandmothers, we might say that receiving unwanted advice makes Granny feel like "a bear with a sore head"—peevish, disgruntled, ill-tempered. The first printed reference to this phrase seems to have been in the October 26, 1824, *Cincinnati Gazette*, wherein a "fatwitted Irishman" was described as "raving around . . . like a bear with a sore head, ever and anon vociferating corruption." The expression may come from hunters, who learned that shooting a bear in a nonvital part of the head made the animal fighting mad and dangerous . . . a sorehead.

Perhaps the saying was coined by the free trappers, or mountain men, who trapped for beaver in the Rocky Mountains in the early 1800s. A mountain man finding a soreheaded grizzly in his lap, or a pack of Blackfoot warriors surrounding his cookfire, was said to be "gone beaver"—hopelessly done for.

The mountain men had their own way of talking. If a trapper "blacked his face" against someone, he went to war, from the Indian practice of warpaint. To "know poor bull from fat cow" was to realize what was bad and what was good, to understand mountain ways: The trappers considered the meat of a bull buffalo tougher and of poorer flavor than that of a cow. To "know the way the stick floats" meant the same thing and referred to the float-stick attached to a beaver trap, which showed the furbearer's location if it swam away with the device.

Many of the trappers' sayings reflected the uncertainty of their existence. To "go under" was to die; to "rub out"—still with us today—was to kill. To "Green River" a man meant to rub him out with a Green River knife, a heavy-bladed weapon manufactured back East along the Green River in Massachusetts. To "shove it in to the Green River" was to plunge the knife to the hilt, where the manufacturer's trademark was engraved. By extension, to do anything "to the Green River" meant to do it to the fullest.

As sayings go, those given us by the mountain men are relatively new. Consider the admonition "cast not your pearls before swine," which refers to wasting something precious on those unable to appreciate its worth. The message comes from Jesus' Sermon on the Mount: "Give not that which is holy unto the dogs, neither cast your pearls before swine, lest haply they trample them under their feet, and turn and rend you."

Shakespeare's works generated a host of sayings—or, more probably, simply recorded them from the colloquial tongue. An example is "the seamy side," used to describe a character in *Othello* and referring to qualities disagreeable, offensive, or immoral. Its literal meaning is the underside of pieced fabric, which shows rough edges, seams, and stitching not normally visible on the finished product. Our adjective, seamy, comes from this phrase.

Another old slogan is "of the first water." Arab gem traders graded diamonds as first, second, and third water, depending on transparency, color, and luster. A diamond of the first water was a flawless stone. Today, "of the first water" means outstanding, perfect, pure. For some reason, though, we often use it to intensify the negative: "He was a thief of the first water."

Liars tell "cock-and-bull stories." The phrase, rooted in both France and England, has been with us since 1600. Scholars speculate that when farmers heard fables about conversations between barnyard animals, they dismissed the tales as "cock-and-bull stories"—nonsense.

Many comparatives describe the state of being drunk: drunk as a fiddler, drunk as a lord, drunk as a beggar, drunk as a skunk, drunk as a boiled owl, and full as a tick (an Australian expression). Other forms include: in the bag, jug-bitten, pie-eyed, loaded for bear, up to the gills, and three sheets in (not "to") the wind. This last description implies that the drinker is unable to stand without weaving and careening about. The sheets referred to are lines attached to a ship's sails, for holding the canvas taut; many vessels from the early nineteenth century, when this saying arose, had three sails, and if the sheets for all three were loose and flapping in the wind, the ship would lurch uncontrollably.

Something excellent, remarkable, or first-rate is called "the cat's meow." Introduced in the early 1900s, this slogan caught the public's fancy in the Roaring Twenties. "Cat's pajamas" was another phrase of the era; pajamas had just been introduced, and they were considered quite racy apparel. In the Twenties people had fun linking animals' names with inappropriate clothing items or body parts: bee's knees, clam's garters, ant's pants, gnu's shoes, pig's wings, sardine's whiskers.

"Dog days" is an older combination still in wide use. The dog days are the hottest, stickiest days of summer, from about July 3 to August 11. These are the days when Sirius, the Dog Star, rises at the same time as the sun. The name "dog days" (Latin *dies caniculares*) comes from the ancient belief that the Dog Star caused the oppressively hot weather. Later, people believed that dogs were most apt to go mad at this time of the year.

Another weather expression is "raining cats and dogs." The common explanation traces to the Norse storm god Odin, who was often depicted with a cat and a dog, creatures then believed to influence the weather. More descriptive is "raining ax handles and pitchforks." During a hard rain, the drops fall straight down and with such force that they look like separate streaks of water—like the tools in the saying. A "three-dog night" popularly describes a frigidly cold night. The phrase comes from the Eskimos, who bring sled dogs into their igloos at bedtime to serve as canine coverlets. A night requiring three dogs is truly a bitter one.

Many sayings are easily traced. "Not worth a Continental"

stems from the time when the fledgling U.S. government issued paper notes without having gold or silver to back up the currency. Merchants refused to accept the notes, called Continentals, rendering them worthless.

Other sayings have never been satisfactorily explained. There are at least five theories, none of them totally convincing, as to why "mind your p's and q's" means to take pains, be careful and precise. To do something quickly is to do it "before you can say Jack Robinson." The expression arose in the late 1700s, but nobody has the slightest idea who Jack Robinson was.

I once heard an elderly friend refer to his neighbor, a redoubtable old woman who singlehandedly ran a cattle ranch, as "a sod widow—not a grass widow, mind you, but a sod widow." A grass widow, it turns out, is a woman separated from her husband by divorce. The term harks back to sixteenth-century England, where it meant an unmarried woman with child, grass apparently alluding to the bed in which the child had been begotten. Sod widow refers to an ordinary widow, one whose husband is under the sod.

We've all been accused at one time or another of crying "sour grapes." The saying comes from Aesop, who illustrated the attitude with a fable. In the story, a fox spotted some grapes dangling from a vine. He jumped and jumped, each time falling an inch short of the luscious fruit. Finally he gave up and waxed philosophical: The grapes were probably sour anyway.

Looking further into the subject of futility, we find, barking at the moon; beating one's head against the wall; beating the air (from the New Testament); the blind leading the blind (Jesus' description of the Pharisees); casting stones against the wind; flogging a dead horse; plowing the sands (from Greek legend); spitting in the sea; and going on a wild-goose chase. In Elizabethan England, a wild-goose chase began with a horse race. The rider of the quickest mount was declared the winner and then allowed to lead the losers about wherever he chose to go. The latter followed at regular intervals, like geese in flight.

Without sayings, colloquialisms, and figures of speech, the average person would have a harder time making himself understood. Sayings come from all trades and professions, from royalty and paupers, city and country, churches and bawdy houses. A great many of them—including some of the funniest—are vulgar. Trying to bar them from this essay has kept the writer between the devil and the deep blue sea. The editor, knowing that most writers are as independent as hogs on ice, undoubtedly kept his eyes peeled. Finding no ribaldry, he's probably in seventh heaven.

The Power of Flies

Rocky Mountain meadows are a great proving ground for fly-killing methods. I developed this one after hours of experimenting: Let the fly land; slide the hand along your leg, index finger raised; when in range, drop the finger quickly. Confident of its speed and unimpressed by the single digit, the fly will be crushed. Joy—until a dozen flies begin vying for the space left by their demolished comrade.

I do not normally spend my time killing flies, but I'd been goaded into it. That summer I was bitten by blackflies, harried by horse flies, punctured by punkies, and driven to instability by stable flies. In four far-flung regions of the continent, I had donated blood to mosquitoes. I was beleaguered and beset, pierced, penetrated, and perforated. Hardly a square inch of my skin went unscathed by the airborne hordes.

My attackers were all flies.

A fly is a member of a large clan of insects that develop from legless maggots or wrigglers and have, as adults, only one pair of wings, evolution having reduced the second pair to stubby flight stabilizers, called halteres. Despite their names, dragonflies, fireflies, and mayflies are not true flies—they have four wings and live completely different lives. The common housefly is a true fly. So is the robber fly, soldier fly, bee fly, midge, mosquito, gnat, and many, many others.

Flies can really fly. What other creature is named for the thing it does best? We don't call a bird "fly," a fish "swim," or a deer "run." As well as being skillful, a creature must be ancient, ubiquitous, prolific—and powerful—to earn so elemental a name.

Harold Oldroyd, senior fly specialist at the British Museum, has probably examined more flies than anyone else in the world. He speculates that today's flies—all eighty thousand species of them—represent a wide range of stages in the exploitation of food.

Flies probably started out living in, and on, decaying vegetable matter—midges and fruit flies still center their lives on this safe, if limiting, environment. Next, some species progressed to dung. Here the plant cells are crushed and broken, the proteins pre-digested, and much of the water removed. Writes Oldroyd in *The Natural History of Flies*, "From the excreta of vertebrates it is a short step to attacking the vertebrates themselves. First nasal and other fluids, discharges from wounds or sores, dead cells, pus," (the screwworm fly lays eggs in running sores, and its maggots go on to devour healthy flesh) "[and] then a gradual transition to lacerating living tissue."

One of the best tissue-laceraters is the stable fly, the creature I learned to crush in the Rockies. The stable fly looks like a house fly clasping a long, tapering awl against its belly. It lands on exposed flesh, jams in the awl, and quickly sucks blood through an opening in the end of the tool. The bite feels like a campfire coal blown against the skin. The bitten spot turns red, swells, and itches.

Stable flies like to go for the legs. Backpackers' shanks and fishermen's ankles are favorite targets. Quick as lightning, stable flies can bite and be gone, dodging the hand, depriving you of the small satisfaction of ending their miserable lives. Stable flies, too, are likely to distract you in some of the most beautiful country imaginable. I met them at nine thousand feet among the breccia-and-sandstone peaks of Wyoming's Absaroka Range. I might as easily have found them in Nova Scotia, on Isle Royale, or on the Baja Peninsula.

Both male and female stable flies drink blood. Among most

96

other biting flies, the males are shy and retiring, sipping nectar and plant juices. It is the females who go out for blood—they need the protein to provision their eggs for hatching.

Another winged nuisance is the blackfly. This diminutive, humpbacked monster locates its prey by sight, by sensing body heat, or by detecting carbon dioxide exhaled with the breath. Writes Oldroyd, "Blackflies are remarkably persistent in their attacks, and surround their victim as a milling cloud. The females often fly round one's legs, and settle at about knee-level, and if one is wearing shorts the knees are soon covered with spots of blood from the bites."

Following her meal, a female blackfly finds a rushing stream. She darts in and out of the water, laying her eggs on plants, rocks, and sticks. After hatching, the larvae clamp onto underwater objects by means of suction cups, silken threads, or fine hairs, depending on their species. The current whirls microscopic plants and animals past them, and the larvae sweep these edible items into their mouths with minuscule, fan-shaped scoops. As a larva matures, it wraps itself in a silk cocoon and begins collecting oxygen from the foam. Soon the cocoon splits. Out pops a bubble, which rises to the surface, bursts, and liberates a blackfly to the bloodthirsty swarm.

In northern Canada, where swamps, rivers, and streams provide a perfect breeding habitat, blackflies may blot out the sun. Their constant biting makes the short summer miserable for warm-blooded creatures. Over ten thousand can be picked off a single cow. Caribou migrate into the wind to escape. Sled dogs dig holes in the dirt and crawl into them. A Canadian entomologist estimated that an unprotected human would lose half his blood to blackflies in less than two hours.

Blackfly bites transmit avian malaria, which can kill up to half of the waterfowl hatched in a local area. Black ducks, wood ducks, mergansers, goldeneyes, and teal periodically suffer high death rates. The loon is hectored by its very own blackfly species; sensors in the insect's legs, which dangle in the water as it flies, pick up a trail of body oils left by the swimming bird—the fly follows relentlessly.

Blackfly bites can spread human diseases. An African species, *Simulium damnosum*, transmits a microorganism causing "river blindness," in which the optic nerve degenerates. But a far more dangerous disease carrier—and a pest every bit as persistent as the blackfly—is the mosquito.

The mosquito—the name is Spanish for "little fly"—comes in more than 3,000 species, three-quarters of them living in the tropics. About 160 species inhabit North America north of Mexico, and each of the fifty states has 40 to 60 varieties. Mosquitoes carry malaria; yellow fever; dengue, or breakbone fever; encephalitis; and a nematode which causes elephantiasis, a lymphatic malady that swells the limbs grotesquely. Mosquitoes have killed more people than all the wars in history. At least a million still die from malaria each year, most of them in southern Asia, Africa, and Central and South America.

The mosquito females are the bloodsuckers. After landing, a mosquito does a handstand to bring her mouthparts to bear. She unsheathes a stylus, whose fine teeth slice neatly through the skin. When the stylus hits a capillary, pumps in the insect's head draw out two to three times her weight in blood—nutrition enough for several hundred eggs.

Mosquitoes lay their eggs in water, or in places likely to be flooded—ponds, lakes, ditches, cans, old tires, tree holes. The eggs hang together in rafts, or are dropped singly, like bombs. Larvae, called wrigglers for the way they thrash through the water, are translucent, segmented, bristling creatures. They feed on detritus, diatoms, and algae. In turn, they are gobbled by fish, dragonfly larvae, planarians, leeches, water beetles, and sundry other creatures.

What novelist D. H. Lawrence called a "small, hateful bugle in my ear" comes from slender wings beating up to five hundred times a second. Male mosquitoes flock to the sound, ready to mate. It is possible to lure them to tuning forks vibrating at the proper frequency, and then electrocute them. Unfortunately, female mosquitoes are not attracted, and all the males can never be zapped. "Trapping 95 percent of them," observes entomologist Howard Ensign Evans, "merely awards to the remainder a particularly orgiastic experience, while leaving us with just as many mosquitoes in the next generation."

A smaller version of the mosquito also does its part to make outdoor life interesting: the biting midge, also called a no-see-um, moose fly, gnat, or punkie. Punkies are seldom noticed until they pierce skin. Much of their tiny bodies must be taken up with jaws, judging from the strength of the bite, but I have never checked closely. I prefer reducing them to atoms.

Punkies have piercing probosci, with mandibles like scissor blades. Most active at dusk, early in the morning, and on cloudy, humid days, they swarm about the head, stabbing below the brim of the hat or at the collar's edge. Punkies, it seems, can fly straight through tent screening—some are scarcely a twenty-fifth of an inch in length, with the really large ones measuring a tenth of an inch. They have chutzpah, and a fine sense of irony: given the chance, a punkie will drain plundered blood from a mosquito's swollen abdomen.

At the opposite end of the size scale is the horsefly. This stout, inch-long, green-eyed brute likes to glide in silently and settle like a feather. Writes fly-man Oldroyd, "When such a fly bites, it makes an appreciable hole, and when it withdraws its stylets a drop of blood usually oozes out."

The females persecute horses, cattle, elephants, hippos, crocodiles, lizards, turtles, monkeys, and, of course, humans. Strong fliers, they have been seen overtaking, circling, and touching down on automobiles going forty miles an hour. Little is known about the males, except that they fly high in the air, and now and then plummet down to glance off the water—apparently a high-speed drinking maneuver that puts off predators.

The horsefly's tough, leathery larvae live in wet mud and rotting wood. They eat other insects, worms, snails, crustaceans, even small toads. "A number kept together in one container," notes Oldroyd, "will end up as one big larva."

Closely related to the horseflies are the slightly smaller deer-flies—together, the two groups are known as the gadflies. A deer-fly circles in an ever-tightening path, looking with its brightly colored eyes for just the right place to land and deliver a searing bite: behind the ear, on the side of the neck, on the thin skin of the temple. On backpacking trips it is mildly heartening to keep tally on the number swatted down. You don't get many, though. They seem to realize that the back of the knee is a pretty safe haven on a biped trying to walk with a sixty-pound pack on its back.

In the United States and in other prosperous countries, most contact with the biting flies has become like the gadfly on the hiker's leg: more a nag than a danger. Insecticides keep fly numbers down, and medical treatment isolates those few persons who contract a disease, making fly-borne epidemics unlikely. Control methods, however, may be changing. Many scientists argue that widespread use of poisons presents a hazard more insidious than the insects themselves, and, in any event, the flies are beginning to develop resistance to the chemicals.

In the 1950s and 1960s, entomologists sterilized male screw-worm flies with radiation, and then released them by the billions to disrupt natural breeding. This technique eliminated the species—a major cattle pest—from Curacao, an island in the Caribbean, and from Florida. Similar strategies are being applied the world over. Scientists also fight flies by releasing parasites and predators, and by spreading chemical sterilants and growth-inhibitors.

But flies remain a force to be reckoned with. The mosquito takes its annual toll, horseflies determine the comings and goings of pastoral nomads, and blackflies render the top of our continent unsuitable for most human activities.

In Africa south of the Sahara lives a close relative of the stable fly: the tsetse. The bite of this fly transmits protozoan diseases to animals and man. One disease is nagana, a fatal fever in cattle,

100

horses, sheep, and swine. Another is African sleeping sickness; a person with this illness grows depressed, anemic, lethargic. Finally he sleeps all the time, becoming emaciated and eventually dying. Great epidemics of both diseases periodically sweep the bush.

"Tsetse has determined man's migration routes and settlements, and defended the interior from invasions from the coast," writes Peter Matthiessen in *The Tree Where Man Was Born*. "[It] remains unrivaled as an impediment to human progress in East Africa. Yet there is reason to believe that 'fly,' by eliminating susceptible animals, opened up an ecological niche for ground-dwelling primates and thereby permitted the debut of baboons and man; quite possibly it also discouraged early forms of man that had as much promise as *Homo sapiens*, and very likely more."

An Hour's Hunt

I cross the creek on the fallen log and climb the bank. My boots crump in the snow. I will hunt the cover in the usual manner: the locust hillside, the planted pines, the old logging road, the fallow field, the alders along the spring run, the spring and the old house foundation, and finally the narrow, crabapple-choked hollow tapering to the ridge.

Sweat traces my backbone as I labor through the locusts. Under the snow, dewberry snags my feet. I work the hillside slowly, dislodging snow from barberry clumps with kicks intended to roust bedded game. Not a rabbit, not a grouse, not a chickadee or nuthatch to watch. Even the snow is unmarked.

In the pines, my passage loosens snow that finds my collar. The sky is brilliant between the boughs. I stop, both to see the sky and to play upon the nerves of hiding grouse. The birds, if they are there, will not be bluffed.

The woods road leaves the pines, and I walk among oaks. Dead leaves still on the trees balance tiny burdens of snow. On other hunts I have flushed grouse here, and the shooting was good because it is open; but today the birds are somewhere else. The fallow field yields no game. The alders, skinny gray against the white hills, hold no snow and no grouse. Uphill from the stone foundation, the spring is snowbound; I hear it trickling.

Like a child who has saved his cake icing for last, I look up the hollow. Surely birds are there, under greenbriars or thornapples or

102

in snow beds beneath the crabs. I crook the shotgun between my arm and side and blow on my hands. The sun makes me squint.

The hills enclosing the hollow send my boot noise back at me. I climb, zigzagging, pausing, listening, knowing I will hear it, hearing it, the muffled wing throbs that blossom to a roar as a grouse breaks from its bed under the snow.

The shotgun covers the sound, but the bird is behind branches. Seconds later I glimpse it far downhill, wings set, shifting slightly in the glide.

Another blur roars out. I pivot and go to my knees, and my shot knocks snow from branches. The grouse is flying fast, and another bird goes out and another and I cannot see to shoot.

I wait, on my knees in the snow. I break the shotgun and load the right barrel. I wait for a minute and then stand. White hills ring me. Snow fills the wrinkles in my pants. Flecks of it melt on my hands. Every aspect of life is fresh—as if I, not the grouse, have broken from the opacity of a snow bed into dazzling light.

Upsik and Siqoq

I saw it on a March night, when I went out for wood.

It covered the remnants of the woodpile. It evened up the tin roofs of the sheds. It soothed the wild tops of the apple trees. It capped the locust posts, poised on the fence wires, whitened the latticed cornstalks beyond.

I forgot my stove chores and walked out in it. It fell on my head, my neck. It hissed on the tops of my ears. It fell like a curtain, shutting out all view of the mountains. It silenced.

In the fencerow, it haloed every weed head, cloaked every blackberry cane. Rabbit tracks stippled it, leading on a dead run into the field. Out in the open it was falling fast, covering new-spread manure, healing tractor stitches in the land.

The rabbit tracks joined another set of rabbit tracks. They turned left, turned right, took off on tangents. I looked, but could see no rabbits. Below, around my boots, spring rivulets gleamed like rivers seen from on high—great, meandering rivers with tributaries and floodplains and oxbows and alluvial fans.

The sky was gray and swarming. I had to avert my face, so hard it came. Hard and cold and a little unfamiliar, coming for the first time so late this winter. My feet encased in huge mud overshoes, I turned back for the house.

It was snow, sure enough, but it was the onion snow. When I took off my boots and tiptoed the last steps to the door, I bid it goodbye for the year.

Snow is no rarity in Pennsylvania. Our annual snowfall varies, but usually we get at least 40 inches, enough for making snowmen, skiing, or tracking deer, depending on your bent, and more than enough for shoveling and plowing. The winter of the onion snow was a lean one. Less than a foot fell all season. Two years previous, we had a shade over 100 inches—a winter of gray evenings, silent nights, and deep white dawns.

Snow, like rain, forms in clouds. For it to fall, certain conditions must be met. There must be adequate humidity, sub-freezing temperature, and microscopic nuclei for water vapor to condense about. A nucleus may be a speck of dust from a farmer's field, ash from a power plant, salt spray from the sea.

The form a crystal takes depends on temperature and moisture levels, and the amount of time the crystal spends growing. In general, the more moisture, the closer the temperature to freezing, and the longer the crystal swirls in the cloud, the more intricate it will be. In polar regions, where the supercooled air holds little moisture, complex crystals rarely develop, and snow amounts to little more than powder. Humid conditions give rise to more complicated crystals, including the elegant stellar form widely considered to be the classic "snowflake." Technically speaking, a single crystal of snow is not a flake at all; a flake is an aggregate of up to a hundred crystals, most of them altered by collisions with their fellows. Neither is the star form the one commonly found in nature. Asymmetric and irregular crystals are far more typical.

The person largely responsible for popularizing the star-shaped crystal is W. A. "Snowflake" Bentley, a farmer from Jericho, Vermont. Around the turn of the century, Bentley made over six thousand microscopic photographs of snow. In 1931 he published a book, *Snow Crystals*, with over two thousand of his pictures. There are six-armed stars (the hexagon is the natural crystalline shape of water) like Belgian lace, stars that are feathered, jeweled, filigreed. While family resemblances show among Bentley's crystals, no two look exactly alike, reinforcing the adage that no snowflake ever has a twin. (Bentley's portrait is in the book. A lean,

105

long-nosed chap in greatcoat and fedora, he bends over a machine that resembles neither a camera nor a microscope but is in fact both—the device he used during thousands of cold, tedious sessions in pursuit of his passion.)

As a snow crystal grows in a cloud, it gets heavier. It may become a perfect subject for a Bentley portrait, or it may take one of many other configurations; it may be battered and broken. Finally, gravity calls it to earth.

In the 1950s, the International Commission on Snow and Ice classified the many forms of falling snow. They named seven basic shapes: star, plate, needle, column, column with a cap at each end, spatial dendrite, and irregular. Later, mainly to pigeonhole the irregulars, C. Magano and C. U. Lee designated over one hundred types of snow crystals, making fine distinctions such as solid bullet, hollow bullet, pyramid, cup, column with dendrites, and so on.

Snow on the ground is at least as diverse and dynamic as snow in the air. Right after a storm, crystals may make up no more than 2 percent of the mass of a snow layer; the rest will be air. Different-shaped crystals fit together differently: granules and needles interlock, stars lie loose and fluffy.

Wind tumbles the crystals against one another. Arms shatter, spikes snap, small crystals lose molecules to larger ones. The snow settles, becoming denser. It is now "old snow." If air can circulate through the snow, as on steep, irregular slopes, then crystals shaped like cups may form. They usually occur in the middle or lower layers of a snowpack, and have the nasty habit of sliding when the upper layers grow too heavy. This is one of the ways snow can avalanche.

In high mountains, old snow may be buried by many storms. It compacts and hardens, becoming *firn*—a German word meaning "last year's snow"—and, if the process completes itself, glacial ice. Snowfalls and pressures needed for such a transformation are difficult for flatlanders to imagine, but the high country truly is snow country. Consider two statistics. In April 1921, a storm dumped 76 inches of snow on Silver Lake, Colorado, in twenty-four hours. During the winter of 1970-1971, Paradise, Washington, on the slope of Mount Rainier, got 1,027 inches.

Snow numbers can be impressive. A foot of snow with average moisture content weighs over a hundred tons to the acre. An inch will drench an acre with the equivalent of twenty-seven hundred gallons of water. The average house roof will collect over twenty thousand pounds in a storm. From a fifty-foot stretch of sidewalk five feet wide, a shoveler removes a ton of white stuff for every 15 inches that fall. And, according to the mathematical contortions of a meteorologist, throughout time enough snow has fallen to mantle the planet fifty miles deep.

A lot of crystals. So many, that scientists doubt the belief that no two are alike. In short, the odds favor duplication—considerable duplication, Snowflake Bentley's photographs notwithstanding. We should also lay to rest the notion that snow is white. It is clear. Transparent snow crystals act as tiny prisms, breaking light into all colors of the spectrum. The human eye, unable to cope with the barrage, gives up and sees the snow as white.

Among humans, no group is as familiar with snow as the Eskimos. Across the top of the world from Greenland to Alaska, they live with snow for all but a few months of the year. Their language reflects the intimacy. Eskimos phrase the question "How old are you?" by asking "How many snows-there-is-none have you seen?" Their language has different words for over two dozen kinds of snow: fresh snow is *api*; snow picked up by wind and deposited in a firm mass is *upsik*; snow skittering along the ground is *siqoq*. Eskimos have special words for fluffy snow that falls without wind, wet springtime snow, crusted early-morning snow that follows a frigid night, dry and sugary snow, snow in long tapered drifts, snow in rounded smooth drifts, snow suitable for igloo building, and more.

Northern animals are equally at home in snow. A deer's winter coat—each hair a hollow, air-filled tube—insulates so well that snow will lie unmelted on the animal's back. Grouse are superbly equipped. As days shorten toward winter, scales on the edges of a grouse's toes begin to lengthen, becoming a fringe that nearly doubles the surface area of each foot: snowshoes. When snow covers nuts and berries, grouse flap into trees and feast on buds. If the snow is dry and powdery they sleep beneath it, flying directly into a snowbank at dusk or sitting at the base of a tree and letting a new snowfall cover them. Otters are inspired by snow. They romp, roll, and bellywhop in it, skidding down hardpacked slides into creeks and lakes. Bears are not above sliding where a suitable slope presents itself. The stolid—some would say stupid—porcupine remains unmoved, paying no more heed to snow than it does to anything else.

Life goes on apace in and under the snow. Algae, fungi, bacteria, rotifers, protozoans, worms, and springtails (also known as snow fleas) live in snows of various regions. Under the snow at ground level, mice and voles dig tunnel networks where they live out the winter. This quiet, dark underworld is full of peril. Weasels, with their long sinuous bodies, travel swiftly through the tunnels. Foxes trotting on a thin crust above are alert to rodent rustlings; standard vulpine technique calls for a graceful leap in the air, front paws breaking through to a tunnel, and a quick snap of the jaws.

Often we speak of a "blanket of snow"—an apt phrase, for snow traps warmth in the ground, protects against frigid air, and moderates drastic changes in temperature. Snow insulates the roots of plants that will send up new life when spring arrives. It provides the soil with nutrients—sulphates, calcium, potassium, nitrates. French farmers say that a healthy February snowfall is worth a load of manure.

Snow can be kind to the land in other ways, I learned one September in Wyoming's Bighorn Mountains. Preparing to hike up a mountain called Cloud Peak, two friends and I camped in an alpine meadow dotted with boulders.

We crowded into the tent soon after supper. Clouds rolled in, and sleet ticked the nylon. My companions drifted off to sleep, but I lay awake thinking about the land. It was yellow with aspens and scrub willows in their fall change, green with gnarled fir. Its lakes were clear and blue. It had shown us elk, deer, and eagles, set off by splendid peaks—but it had seen too much of man.

Fire rings, trash piles, range cattle, and eroded trails greeted us at every turn. We met a forest ranger who told us that at least three hundred people had climbed Cloud Peak that summer. The trail to its summit muddied the meadow where we camped.

As I lay in my sleeping bag, I heard the ticking on the tent give way to a gentle hiss. I must have dozed, because later, when I peered out, the ground was white. I put on boots and parka and went outside.

The snow crunched under my feet. Somewhere rocks slid, the clatter muffled by falling snow. I took shelter under the lip of a mammoth boulder. In the meadow, the snow had erased the trail. The tent was a white hump, another boulder capped with snow.

Stolen Moments

Living in the woods, I can usually steal a moment or two each day. I spend a quarter-hour sitting on the edge of the meadow in the moonlight. I walk up to the gate before leaving for the office. I grab ten minutes to pick caterpillars off the black walnut sapling. I always keep my eyes and ears open; with time so short, I don't want anything to pass unnoticed.

Last night, after work and after working for a while on the house (nothing, by the way, can eat up free time faster than building your own home), I stole a moment. Dusk was coming on. I walked up to the township road, turned right for a few hundred yards, and turned right again, onto a grassy lane that separates our woods from the logged-over land. I walked down to our southeast corner and followed the road where it hooks back across our land toward Oak Pond. My standard route.

I pad along in sneakers and shorts, avoiding the blackberry shoots that push up through the grass. Ahead, a gangly doe in her red summer coat browses on sassafras. She winds me and bounces off the lane, white tail whipping. Going on, I see a yellow slime mold draping an oak stump. A pile of bear droppings (full of seeds; where the bear lucked into ripe raspberries is anybody's guess). A towhee: Its wings break the stillness—a burst of six beats, a pause, half a dozen more.

I am lifting a fallen limb clear of the trail when something flies at me. It comes down the center of the lane, three feet off the ground. It is dark brown and headless. The creature hangs in the air about ten feet away, tail down and long wings pumping; the wind from its wings buffets the ferns below. It lands on a leaning stick, its body lengthwise to the perch. A whippoorwill.

The bird utters a rapid *whick-whick-whick*. It flies to the ground, spreads its wings and tail, and makes a low, roaring growl. The call is ventriloqual: I fight down the impulse to look around and see if a bird is going to smack me from behind.

I know from the way the bird is acting that it has a nest nearby. I look in the laurel. I take a step, checking the ground before setting my foot. The bird flutters past my face, and I glimpse the broad, foreshortened head and gaping mouth. I find a flattened spot in the leaves, with droppings scattered about. After another tentative step, I spot the chicks.

They are two, squatting side by side in identical postures, like a finely feathered toad beside a mirror. A male whippoorwill calls from the woods; the light is failing fast. It seems incredible that in two weeks' time, these two will fly.

I brought my notebook outside today. I walked about a hundred yards from the house and sat against an oak. Gypsy moths—the miserable, leaf-eating caterpillar stage is past—flutter through the woods. This has not been a particularly bad year for the pests; the population was low, and the caterpillars were afflicted with a strange lethargy that caused many to die before reaching full size, and others not to emerge from their pupae. Still, male moths by the dozens flit erratically through the forest, searching for females.

I am startled by a *yank*. I can't pinpoint what made it. It sounds like a hen grouse calling her chicks. My eyes search the knee-high huckleberries, but find nothing. *Yank*—from straight above. I raise my head. A nuthatch clings to the trunk. It looks me in the eye. It scoots around to the back of the tree, sending bits of bark floating down onto my head, and takes off.

Until last night, it had been over a month since we'd had any substantial rain. Dust lay deep along the berm of the road, and the streams trickled. The raspberries were little green fists. (It comes to me, now, where the bear must have gotten his berries: near water, and the closest water is the small stream toward whose upper reaches I am heading right now.)

Last night it rained hard. The rain came in bursts, drumming the tin roof; thunder rumbled, far enough away not to set me squirming, close enough to make me snuggle into the blankets. Now, at half past six in the morning, I am starting down the township road to pick up yesterday's mail.

Each leaf glistens. The tree trunks are dark and wet. An orange sun angles through the woods, and a patch of blue shows between gray clouds. The top of the mountain is covered by cloud; the blue gap closes and a light rain starts to fall.

Out in the cutover land, I pass the nest of a blue-gray gnatcatcher. I spotted the cup—woven onto an upward-angling branch near the top of an oak—soon after it had been built in early May. I suppose the bird thought the tree would leaf out. It will never green again: killed by the gypsy moth. Even if unexpected, the lack of a canopy apparently did not deter the gnatcatcher; I could see its tail sticking out of the cup for several weeks as it brooded. Then I did not walk the road for a month, and now the nest looks empty.

A catbird squalls from the brush, tangled locust and aspen and blackberry and sumac and elderberry competing to cover the stumps. The breeze smells clean and sweet. Deer tracks mark the mud beside the road. Something crashes through the brush on the other side.

You can steal moments very nicely in the rain. My neighbor puts on a slicker and hip boots and walks all over the country when it rains. He sees a lot; his eye is practiced and he knows the land well. It hurt him to see the logging. It was the second time he had seen the trees cut, and it will be the last. The first time they used horses to skid the logs, he told me, and moved their mill with its steam-powered saw to the timber.

112

Not much mail. A bank statement and a letter from a group called Friends of the Earth, asking for money to fight "James Watt and the energy giants." "Make no mistake," the letter says. "Watt is cashing in America's greatest assets—but you and I won't see any dividends."

I pocket the letters and turn toward home. I hesitate; decide to check the stream.

Down the bank, and I am among striped maple, tulip poplar, sassafras, and ankle-thick grapevines. Big white oaks and hemlocks push up out of sturdy rhododendrons. The stream dances between mossy rocks, and pools below logs. A frog the size of a penny blips across the bank. I kneel and drink the rain.

Coming up the bank, I find a raspberry bush laden with ripened fruit. I pick a handful and pop them into my mouth. The tang is instant, high and sweet. The seeds crush between my teeth. A red stain marks my palm.

Five feet from the back door, a moth is dying. It quiets in my hand. I go get a lens.

A brown, tubular tongue protrudes from a slit between the moth's bulging eyes; the tongue's tip is covered with tiny hairs—the better to lick up dew, or nectar? The legs, banded brown and tan, are covered with spines. The forewings mix grays, browns, blacks. When lifted, they reveal underwings marked with a double band of red as ruddy as a January sunset. Under my fingers, short rods of pigments fray off, leaving a tan grid.

The breeze takes the moth out of my hand and deposits it in the weeds. I walk among the trees and find a female gypsy moth astride a patch of eggs the size of my thumbnail. The eggs are salmon-colored and coated with tiny tan hairs. The moth has black compound eyes and seems to lack a tongue and mouthparts—perhaps there is no need for feeding in this final stage of life, which lasts only a few days.

I am about to discard this shriveled husk when I catch a green glint. I focus the lens. A wasp, or a fly, strides across the moth's

113

eye. Its wings reflect blue and green and violet. The fly's antennae flicker; its abdomen dips. A brown needle extends from its tail to the gray, matted hair at the base of the moth's eye. I think I see something left behind. An egg.

I may have missed the black raspberries, but blackberries are sweet, and mound quickly in the pail.

I decide to stand in one spot and see how many I can pick. I stop counting at 150. Some of the berries are glossy—the barely ripe ones. Dead-ripe berries have a dull sheen, and drop off at the slightest touch. Relieved of their weight, the canes rock up slowly.

Time spent picking berries, I think, need not be labeled stolen. Berry picking rewards in three ways. It soothes. It keeps you quietly occupied, so you are more apt to see things. It pays you back when you cover a piece of woodstove-toasted bread with sweet jam, and begin to feel, in midwinter, that summer will come again.

Tonight I don't see much. An assortment of bugs, beetles, flies, and caterpillars among the berries and thorns. I hear birds—towhees, wood thrushes, and robins, only the robins singing with anything approaching enthusiasm.

Three quarts in an hour. Not a record, but not bad, either.

My neighbor turned seventy-nine last month. This evening we walk along the township road, and he shows me pennyroyal, horseweed, cudweed, evening primrose. Joe-Pye-weed nods its lavender head; rabbits crouch in the powdery dust, their sides heaving.

We tick off the signs of fall we have been seeing. Beyond the shortening days, there is the goldenrod in flower, and thistles going to seed. Crickets singing at night. The husky chitter of katydids.

My neighbor stops to pull Queen Anne's lace—he calls it wild carrot. He tugs it out of the bank and tosses it in the middle of the road. There was a time, he tells me, when a farmer thought nothing of going out in his fields and weeding. He remembers rainy days when he and his uncle and his grandfather would cull his grandfather's fields; the moist soil gave up the roots easily.

We pass those same fields, now owned by people who live some- where else—Philadelphia, it is said. Goldenrod grows thick. The pale heads of Queen Anne's lace, tight and turning brown, spread throughout the grass.

Expectations

"Blessed is he who expects nothing, for he shall never be disappointed."

Don't ask me who penned this obscure beatitude. Probably some English poet who spent his idle hours slogging through brushy fens after woodcock, or missing easy shots on driven game.

With hunting season upon us, I am reciting the admonition daily. It's no use, of course; I will enter this year's first bird cover just as primed with expectations as I was the autumn before.

For example, this season I expect to shoot more accurately than in the past. (Why, I don't know; I haven't swung on a claybird all summer and have yet to memorize Robert Churchill's classic *Game Shooting*, as I resolved to do after missing a succession of shots on grouse last January.)

This fall, too, I expect to train my keen shooter's eye on bumper crops of grouse, woodcock, pheasants, rabbits, and squirrels. (In reality, the chance of finding more game is slim to nonexistent; it's been years since I did any preseason scouting, and I seem to meet more hunters in my favorite covers every year.)

I expect to do more hunting than in years past. (I'm conveniently ignoring several writing deadlines, a stack of unanswered letters, and the fact that I used three weeks of vacation on a back-packing trip to Wyoming.)

I expect to make my first double on grouse. (It's more luck than skill when I kill two birds the same day, let alone on the same rise.)

Anyway, to really start the juices flowing, I have dug out my gunning vest. Snugged in the shell loops are last year's last rounds, to become this year's first. I pull out my gloves, stiff from repeated rain soakings and scratched by greenbriar and raspberry thorns. I open the game pouch and find apple leaves still faintly green; pine needles; two acorns; half a tooth-marked Milky Way; goldenrod fuzz; corkscrew grape tendrils; a feather from a woodcock's back, a little brown and black plume with a ball of down at its base; and close to a quart of unidentifiable debris. The vest is redolent of old orchards, pine thickets, rain, and birds. Thoroughly intoxicated, I hang it back in the closet, a new and sumptuous expectation of full game pouches and gourmet dinners taking shape in my mind.

I'm not as glib as all this suggests. In addition to my optimistic expectations, I have a great many more realistic ones.

I expect to be outsmarted by game maybe twenty-five times, and to outsmart them maybe twice.

I expect to be drafted into protracted searches for wayward pointers, setters, and hounds.

I expect somebody's bird dog to eat the woodcock I have shot.

I expect one particularly inquisitive fellow to try to worm good bird-hunting locations out of me, and I expect to put him off in a manner more churlish than skillful.

I expect to get so flustered (three grouse flushing from a thicket will do it nicely) that I drop a hammer on an empty chamber, forget which way the safety goes, or sling my shells on the ground.

I expect to run out of ammunition in an out-of-the-way cover that usually holds a grouse or two but today is lousy with woodcock.

I expect to ride in the back of a station wagon next to the dog box after the dog has just rolled in day-old bear dejecta.

I expect to come back from a hunt and have somebody ask, "Did you catch anything?"

I expect the days to shorten, and frost to mow down the weeds. Groundhogs and chipmunks to retreat underground. Woodcock to vacate their boggy haunts by the third week in November, letting me concentrate on grouse. (Invariably, though, I flush an unpunctual timberdoodle, and look like an overanxious batter swinging for a fastball when the pitcher delivered a curve: out in front, off-balance, and sure to miss.)

I can count on a few outstanding days each autumn, days that will seed themselves in my imagination to spring up as next year's expectations. A limit of woodcock in three hours' gunning, after frosty northern nights have driven down the flight birds. A day of shared precision—two hunters, five rifle shots, five squirrels. A clean, swift kill on a yearling doe.

Many days will be special for reasons other than game bagged. I expect some time to catch an animal so completely dead to rights (last year it was a squirrel up a solitary sapling that had shed its leaves; he looked sheepish and dropped the nut he was carrying) that I will crook the gun over one arm, deliver a short lecture on the importance of remaining unseen, and leave the creature to ponder its great good luck.

I expect to be brought up short by the significance of insignificant things. Smooth stones, tan and red and brown, under clear running water. Fog filling a valley. Rainy-day crows silent in bare trees. Blood on my hands: my own, welling from briar furrows, and that of wild animals.

I expect my senses to work overtime. To smell gun oil and powder, wet dogs, leather, snow, mud in the woodcock covers, and maybe even the woodcock themselves, a dun-colored scent that lies beneath the kinnikinnick on bare, chalk-spattered earth. To hear murmurous geese, see their lopsided vees writhing across the sky. To hear faraway shots and the close, metered footfalls of deer. Taste tangy Smokehouse apples off abandoned trees. Feel wind and chill and rain, followed by the warmth of fire.

I remember a rainy day last November when I stood on the edge of a five-acre crabapple patch with great, hanging clusters of grapes and a partner on the other side and a dog somewhere in between.

The dog was ostensibly a pointer and a retriever, but it seemed to function better as a long-range spaniel, flushing grouse well out in front where we did not have to waste ammunition missing them. Earlier, I had rousted a bird myself, and by some fluke knocked it down. The dog had a gleam in its eye, so I hurried over and fetched it myself.

I expected to fill my two-bird limit. Stepping carefully, I conducted my own hunt along the edge of the crabapples. The muted flushing of distant birds told me the dog was hard at work.

Ahead, a tall tree had pitched over in a storm, dragging down vines and uprooting shrubs. I expected a grouse to be sitting somewhere in the tangle. I expected it to flush and fly dead away from me down the corridor left by the fallen tree. I expected to knock it galley west with the improved cylinder barrel of my shotgun.

As I stood looking down the opening, I heard the roar of wings. The grouse powered up. It turned and flew straight at me, flaring to miss my head.

I ducked, stumbled, spun, and threw up the gun. I expected to miss with both barrels, and did.

A Rogues' Gallery of Bats

If you see a bat slipping through the twilight, pick up a pebble and loft it into the air. The bat will hear it. He will dart over to meet the stone at its apogee. He will inspect it, reject it, and go on about his business.

Keep watching, and you will see him catch an insect. (He is not, as you may be, out for an evening stroll; he is having breakfast.) A small insect—a midge or a mosquito—the bat will take directly in his mouth. An insect the size of your pebble—a June beetle—he will disable with a quick bite, cradle in his wings and tail, carry to the ground, and eat there. If his target takes evasive action, the bat will flick out a wing and snag the bug like a shortstop spearing a line drive.

Bats are the only mammals capable of powered flight. (Flying squirrels glide.) The scientific name for the Order of bats is Chiroptera, Latin for "hand-winged." A bat's wings are, in fact, hands whose digits are webbed with thin skin. Each wing has a thumb (a curved claw about halfway out on the wing's leading edge) and four fingers, each like an umbrella rib. Opened, the bones fan out to support a leathery airfoil; closed, they pleat the wing against the body.

In 1794, Lazzarro Spallanzani, an Italian anatomist, got together some bats and some owls. He found that while the owls could not navigate in total darkness, the bats could. When Spallanzani blinded several bats, he was amazed to find that they could still dodge threads hanging in a room, and, released to nature, could fill their stomachs with insects. He found that earplugs rendered the bats helpless. Not until the late 1930s did science discover why. Then, Harvard student Donald Griffiths proved the often-advanced theory that bats make sounds beyond human hearing, and listen to the echoes of these sounds to navigate.

A bat is on the hunt. Cruising, he hums out through his nostrils a beam of sound, ten to twenty high-pitched clicks per second. While most of the clicks vanish into the night, a few bounce back, from tree limbs, leaves, a wire fence. The clicks reach the bat's ears, and he steers clear of the obstructions.

A pulse strikes a moving object and returns. Instantly the bat lowers the pitch of his sound stream, directs it at the object, and increases the number of clicks per second. The sounds return, but at an even lower pitch: The object is moving away. The bat flaps his wings, picks up speed. As he closes with the target, he lowers the pitch of his sound yet another notch—so low that a human observer with acute hearing might detect a very high, fast ticking. The bat flies down the trail of echoes. He nets a moth in one wing and folds it to his body. He gulps down thorax and abdomen, letting the insect's head fall and its wings flutter to the ground.

A bat is grace and alacrity on the wing. Up close, it elicits from most people the same feelings as does a man with a conspicuous deformity: revulsion, and curiosity.

As a boy, if I wanted to throw a good scare into myself, I would open the *World Book* to "Bats." One page was a veritable rogues' gallery. Bats with ribbed ears, spear-shaped snouts, pinhead eyes, needle teeth. Bats with faces like hogs'. Bats with the long skulls of horses, bats like lizards and sheep and old prizefighters and Martians and foxes and medieval Satans. Bats have not bothered to change their appearances in the intervening years. The grotesquery has a purpose: Flaring ears capture sounds and get rid of excess heat. Spear-shaped noses direct echolocation pulses. Tiny eyes fit a streamlined head.

When I got out the *World Book*, I used to imagine those ruddy gargoyles leaping off the page, attaching themselves to my neck, and sucking blood. Most people fear bats in ways no more rational than my boyhood imaginings. People believe bats will attack them. Most bats are rabid. Bats get caught in women's hair. Bats are filthy, and their guano is a dangerous source of tuberculosis and other diseases.

In fact, bats are no more apt to be rabid than are foxes, skunks, or other wild animals. Bats never tangle themselves in women's hair. Or men's hair. They are too adept at flying. Bats do not attack people; people who get bitten have usually picked up a sick bat lying on the lawn. Even the western mastiff bat—a denizen of the Southwestern desert and the largest bat in North America—is no bigger than a screech owl. The mastiff does not seize small children, or even toy poodles. It eats, according to the experts, "rather small insects."

Bats are among the cleanest of animals—like birds, they must groom themselves frequently or risk diminishing their ability to fly. In only one case have bats been found to have tuberculosis; the investigators speculated that the disease was an avian strain contracted from vultures sharing the cave. No one has uncovered evidence that bats, or their droppings, transmit tuberculosis to man.

Bats inhabit tropical and temperate regions around the globe. There are bent-winged bats and disc-winged bats. Sucker-footed bats, sheath-tailed bats, free-tailed bats, wrinkle-faced bats. Leaf-chinned, leaf-nosed, long-nosed, lump-nosed, broad-nosed, and tube-nosed bats. Fringe-lipped bats. Hollow-faced bats and hammer-headed bats. Pallid, spotted, funnel-eared, big-eared, long-eared, long-legged, long-tongued, and small-footed bats. One in every five species of mammals is a bat. The vast majority have no vernacular names.

Despite the fact that all bats are built along the same basic lines, they eat very different foods. All of the North American species subsist mainly on insects, although a few of the larger ones are not above picking off their smaller relatives. Elsewhere in the world are bats that eat fish, frogs, lizards, rodents, birds, fruit, and, yes, blood.

The fishing bat possesses large feet with sharp, hooked claws. It swoops low across the water, legs dangling, skimming echolocation cries off the surface. When a fish breaks the water, it reflects sound. The bat zeroes in and gaffs the fish with its claws.

Bats that feed on fruit, nectar, and pollen inhabit the world's tropics. Some of these bats have large, round eyes (they maneuver by sight, and not by echolocation) and canine physiognomies, and are known as flying foxes. Robust animals, they weigh up to two or three pounds, and one type has wings spanning nearly six feet. The tricolored short-tailed fruit bat, a Caribbean species, possesses the indelicate habit of defecating when forced to fly an abrupt turn, spattering houses and people. Some of the larger species are highly sought for food, and their numbers are declining throughout much of their range—an ominous turn, since many are important plant pollinators.

The vampire bat ranges through South and Central America. A vampire is small—about three inches long, with a five-inch wingspan. At night, it flies in search of a horse, cow, pig, or human. Like the insect-eaters, the vampire uses echolocation to find prey, but the sound pulses are tuned to a lower frequency to better identify a larger target. The bat lands near a sleeping victim and crawls aboard. Using its upper incisors, it shaves a shallow cut, and then laps and sucks the blood that wells from the wound. A component of the bat's saliva inhibits clotting, letting the bat drink its fill. A vampire consumes about forty-six pints of blood a year. The species rarely feeds on humans; when it does, the point of attack is commonly the big toe.

Enough of foreign bats. The bats in our own woods and fields and chicken coops are exotic enough themselves.

A day in the life of a little brown bat—the garden variety bat found across the top of the continent—begins around sunset. The bat stirs and bickers a bit with her neighbors (bat writers invariably describe commotion in the colony as bickering), detaches her feet from the roof of the hideaway, and, with a wingbeat or two, rights herself and flits out into the evening air.

She heads for a nearby pond, flies low, and scoops up water with her lower jaw. She begins to feed, picking up gnats, flies, beetles, and moths, following a set hunting path, a narrow loop perhaps twenty yards across. She feeds for an hour, at a rate approaching one capture every seven seconds, accumulating one-fifth of her body weight in insects. She rests in a tree for a time, then feeds again. At dawn, she returns to the roost.

In late spring, female little brown bats form nursery colonies of a dozen to over a thousand individuals. They congregate in attics, barns, and other hot, dark places. Each mother bears a single baby. The nursery's hot temperature—up to 130 degrees F—spurs growth of the young, which can fly after only three or four weeks. Male bats also seek out dark daytime retreats: rock crevices, spaces behind shutters, attics. It is this habit of shunning the light that launched a strange episode of human-bat interaction.

It was 1941, and the Japanese had just attacked Pearl Harbor. Dr. Lyle Adams, a surgeon from Irwin, Pennsylvania, thought about retaliation. Adams reasoned that bats could be fitted with time-bombs and dropped over enemy cities, factories, and military bases. The bats would hide in cracks and crannies. Hours later, the explosives would detonate, igniting thousands of fires. Adams sold his plan to the military and was told to proceed.

Scientists on the project, code-named "X-Ray," determined that bats could carry three times their weight. The western mastiff could lug a one-pound stick of dynamite, but there weren't enough mastiffs to do the job. The pallid bat, another western species, could carry three ounces, but was not hardy enough to withstand crating and parachute release. The team finally settled on the free-tailed bat, which inhabits Southwest desert caves by the millions. The scientists captured hundreds of thousands of bats. They designed refrigerated containers to hold one thousand to five thousand chilled, lethargic bats. To each bat they strapped a one-ounce incendiary that delivered a twenty-two-inch flame for eight minutes. They tested their handiwork by bombing a dummy village; it burned to the ground. Escaped bats also set fires that consumed an auxiliary air base at Carlsbad, New Mexico.

X-Ray never saw action. In 1944, the $2 million project was abruptly abandoned. Adams believed the military made a mistake. "We found that bats scattered as much as twenty miles from the point where the bombs opened," he said later. "Think of thousands of fires breaking out simultaneously over a circle forty miles in diameter. Japan could have been devastated."

The bat caves of the Southwest, where X-Ray scientists captured their subjects, are well known; some are called "smoke holes" for the way dark clouds of bats issue from their mouths at dusk. In their book *Bats of America*, Roger Barbour and Wayne Davis describe a visit to a huge colony of free-tailed bats: "The bats are always alert, and the disturbance of the intruder's lights causes them to peel off from the great clusters in rapidly increasing numbers until the case is filled with hordes of milling bats. The floor and the walls of the cave soon seem to be crawling with them, and they collide with the observer . . . They cling to him and crawl upward to reach a high point from which to launch into flight. A writhing mound of bats quickly accumulates and, although they make no effort to bite, one gets the feeling that he may be smothered by the animals as he sinks deeper into the loose and sometimes soggy guano which covers the cave floor."

Caves are vital to many North American bats. In the north of the continent, bats flock to caves in the fall. Here, insulated by the earth, they sit out the cold, insect-barren winter. In the still, humid atmosphere, the bats hook their feet into the ceiling and hibernate. Most species favor cave zones having the lowest stable temperature above freezing, a condition under which their metabolic processes burn fat at the minimum rate. Over the course of the winter, the bats wake up and move to new chambers as temperatures change—with each move, consuming more of their precious fat.

Commercializing a cave usually ruins it for the bats which may have been wintering there for centuries. Cave explorers, or spelunkers, also disturb bats, often without realizing it. Consider the case of the Indiana bat, on the U.S. Endangered Species List. This close cousin of the little brown bat likes to hibernate near the mouths of caves, where it is vulnerable to every intrusion. To make matters worse, Indiana bats roost cheek-to-jowl, forming brown patches like bee swarms on the cavern roofs. When a bat on the fringe of the cluster is awakened, it moves about, starting a ripple of activity that spreads throughout the swarm. A winter of repeated disturbances may kill many colony members.

Bat populations rebound slowly from setbacks, as birthrates are low: Most species bear only one young each year. Bats succumb to natural dangers—owls and rat snakes and raccoons and foxes, cold weather, the occasional shortage of insects, a flooded cave. People pose a greater threat. Inspired by fears of rabies and tuberculosis, people have dynamited bat caves. When colonies are deemed a nuisance—as in a homeowner's attic—poison sprays are brought out. Poisoning is a dangerous tactic, since the toxins tend to filter into human living space, and sick bats—on the lawn, in the shrubbery—are far more likely to come into contact with people and pets. Better to exclude the bats. Plug cracks and screen off vents, in the fall when young and adults have flown away to hibernate.

This last bit of advice comes from Bat Conservation International. BCI, as the organization calls itself, organized in 1982. Members are dedicated to protecting bat habitat around the world, and to reforming bats' images. BCI reviews books on bats, including *Bats? Relax. They're Really Very Nice;* and *Bats of America*, by Barbour and Davis—"The information is good, but many photos unfortunately show bats snarling defensively."

You can become a member for $25 a year, $500 for life. Dr. Merlin D. Tuttle, curator of mammals at the Milwaukee Public Museum, directs the group's American branch.

I wrote to Dr. Tuttle. He sent me plans for a bat house.

126

Sleeping Out

My friend Norman Dodd tells about a time he slept out unexpectedly. In the 1930s, he was a big-game guide in the Absaroka Mountains of Wyoming. One crisp autumn day he went elk hunting alone. Dusk found him far from his cabin. The route back was too treacherous with stream crossings, too complicated with fallen timber, for a horse to negotiate at night.

Dodd rode to a creek, where he unsaddled his horse and turned it loose to graze. He gathered driftwood from the water's edge and deadfall from the darkening forest, heaped the wood on a sandbar by the stream, and lit the pile. The fire brightened the walls of trees enclosing the stream. The moon glinted off the swift water. Coyotes yapped.

For an hour Dodd sat in the sand, a horse blanket over his shoulders, feeding wood to the blaze. When the fuel was gone and the fire low, he kicked the embers into the stream. With a stick he dug in the steaming sand, scooping out a narrow trench. He folded his blanket onto the bottom, lay down, and pulled a second blanket on top of him. Enclosed by heat radiating from the sand, he slept.

I have never slept on a sandbar, but I have spent many nights out-of-doors—comfortable, miserable, revealing, seemingly interminable, pacifying, nerve-wracking nights.

Most of those nights were spent in a tent. The most palatial was a boxy wall tent that you could stand in. We broke a couple of hay bales onto the floor. A sheepherder's stove squatted in the corner; loaded with oak chunks, it gave off heat enough to make a down sleeping bag too warm for comfort, even though it was December and snow covered the ground. (In retrospect, I realize that we had placed ourselves in a terrifyingly dangerous situation: A spark in the hay, and the whole tent could have turned into an inferno.)

I started camping when I was a boy, almost twenty years ago. Then, tents bore little resemblance to the lightweight, airy, secure structures they are today. A friend resurrected a musty canvas car-camper that belonged to his grandfather; our parents drove us to camping spots because the tent was too heavy to carry. When it rained, we could flick the ceiling with a finger and start a minor shower inside. The walls tied down, but not tightly. One night a raccoon entered. According to my friend, it sauntered down the space between us, climbed onto my chest, sniffed my nose, and climbed down again. He prodded it out of the tent with a flashlight.

Later, my parents bought an umbrella tent, a pyramidal affair constructed from yard upon yard of green canvas. As far as I know, they never slept in it. This tent, too, traveled best on wheels. One time a friend and I drove it to Assateague Island, off the coast of Virginia. We set it up, a rainstorm knocked it down, we set it up again, a swarm of greenhead flies forced their way inside, followed by clouds of mosquitos, we pulled our sleeping bags out of the tent, considered burning it or leaving it there for some other unfortunates, decided not to risk my parents' wrath, stuffed the tent into the trunk of the car, and, that same night, drove home.

When I was about eighteen, I acquired a contraption called a tube tent. To set it up, I inflated a triangle of plastic tubes; these formed a rigid entrance through which I could crawl into a tapering, plastic pouch. The arrangement kept out rain, but sealed in vapor. When I breathed, the tent filled with moisture-laden air; the moisture condensed on the tent's walls and ran down onto my sleeping bag, soaking it.

The tube tent concept fell by the wayside as a new generation of nylon tents evolved. I own a mountain tent that weighs less than ten pounds and boasts a cooking alcove, breathable top and sides, a watertight fly that sits suspended above the entire structure, with a dozen stakes and a maze of cords for anchoring the system down. The tent resists snow, torrential rain, and gusts that would have made short work of the old green pyramid.

Sleeping in a tent you trust is a pleasant experience. In recent summers, a friend and I have backpacked in the Rocky Mountains. Each time we took his tent. It is a dome tent, of a style that promises to supplant the coffin-shaped, steep-ridged mountain tents that have become so popular in recent years. The tent is roomy and well-ventilated. Although larger than mine, it weighs less. With an aluminum frame that curves over it on the outside, the tent need not be staked down—the weight of its occupants secures it. Empty, it can be lifted up and moved until the softest, levelest site is found.

The tent perched in a clearing like a green-and-yellow spacecraft. My friend, who sells wilderness travel equipment for a living, would marvel at the tent's efficiency and beauty, and question the judgment of anyone who might own any other kind. So often did he praise the tent that I began hoping, in a perverse way, that a seam would open during a thunderstorm, or that the tent might, as we watched from afar, be borne on a wind over a precipice. (I heard about one such accident. A hiker pitched his tent on the slick rocky summit of Half Dome in Yosemite Park. In the night, when he went out to relieve himself, a gust picked up his tent and sent it wheeling into the pines several thousand feet below. He retrieved it in the morning. For the rest of the night, though, no tent or sleeping bag.)

My friend's tent worked well. The only time trouble threatened was during a snowstorm. That night, I wakened to the whisper of flakes. I dozed, and when I woke again the tent was sagging overhead. I considered this situation, got out of my bag, pulled on boots, and went out to brush off a foot of powder. The next day we met a solitary traveler. He reported that he had slept through the storm until his tent collapsed on top of him. Even then, he said, he barely wakened. He speculated that he might have died if he hadn't finally roused himself: The snow could have sealed his tent around him so tightly that he would have suffocated.

When the weather permits it, the best outdoor sleeping is had without a tent. With no walls or ceiling to hold it out, the night embraces you. Dew dampens your shoulders. Breezes carry scents—the hay smell of ferns, ocean salt, the damp, black breath of humus. Bugs must be tolerated, but, in return, you earn the glow of foxfire and sudden streaks of shooting stars. You waken at first light, drift back to sleep, waken, drowse again. After catnapping for an hour, you feel as if you have slept very late when, in fact, you rise earlier than you ever get out of bed at home.

Before the outdoor magazines developed a fixation for telling us how to do everything, they used to run adventure stories. Many were illustrated with drawings of rough-featured men lying back in their sleeping bags, fingers laced behind their heads, coffee pots on the fire, Winchesters at their sides. These, I knew, were real men. They disdained tents. Nor did they bother to stretch the covers of their sleeping bags over a framework of sticks, to make little shelters for their faces, as did the cleancut men in the Sears catalog.

My friends and I admired the real men. We would take our .22s and sleeping bags, and go sleep under the stars. One evening three of us camped in a pine woods near home. We spread our bags on a heap of dry pinecone scales—built a fire, told stories, drifted off to sleep. At dawn, I wakened to a blow on my shoulder. My companions lay motionless, wormed deep in their bags. A chattering rang out overhead. As I looked through the branches of a tree, a pinecone came hurtling through the dim light, whacking limbs, dislodging needles, and landing with a thump beside my head. I spotted a red squirrel on a limb. Its tail whipped up and down, scolding us.

I had been cold all night; I was still cold, and I knew I would not be able to get back to sleep. I eased my hand out of the bag and found my .22. A box of cartridges lay nearby, and I fished one out. I loaded, closed the bolt gently. My friends still slept. I aimed at the squirrel and pulled the trigger. The shot echoed through the woods, and my friends' wide-eyed faces came popping out of their bags. I had missed. Breakfast time.

We slept cold too often back then. Many nights I would waken in the dark, shivering and bladder-full, wishing for morning, swearing that I would never sleep out again. Mercifully, down came into my life. Down—the soft, fluffy underfeathers of birds, most notably ducks and geese. Down—if you kept it dry, it would keep you warm. Now, I could sleep outside in January. Down was light, compressible (you could jam a whole sleeping bag into a bread sack), and, when I learned about it, inexpensive, not yet having been seized upon by fashion designers for stuffing the coats of society women and college students.

I own two down sleeping bags—a one-pounder for summer, and a two-pounder for spring and fall. For winter camping, the summer bag slips inside the heavier mummy.

Mummy bags are comfortable, but not for the claustrophobic. A jammed zipper will imprison you in warmth all night. You cannot move swiftly from the confines of a mummy bag. One time in the Rockies, we camped in a tiny bowl surrounded by cliffs. That night, the temperature dropped, freezing water in the cliffs, breaking rocks loose. We lay trussed up like pigs in blankets, listening to the boulders clacking, praying that the slides would peter out before they reached us.

On several recent trips, I've carried a rain poncho that doubles as a tent. By adding a few light aluminum poles, and running lines to nearby trees, I can fashion a sturdy awning. A new product, touted as the ultimate personal shelter, is the so-called bivouac or "bivvy" sack, a nylon envelope that zips around your sleeping bag. I considered buying one, but it looked too much like a tube tent.

Most nights that we sleep outdoors, we pitch a tent just in case, spread a plastic sheet and a foam pad on the ground outside, and fluff up the mummy bags. We snuggle into our warm cocoons as the wind dies, the stars sharpen, and the temperature plummets.

Often we lie awake and trade stories. I like to tell the one about my old friend, the hunting guide, who, with his ingenuity, turned a sandbar into a warm, inviting bed. I never tell the whole story, though. In the middle of the night, he got cold. Had to get up and huddle by a fire until dawn.

Crow

I was hunting morels on a May morning when I heard a fight boil up in the pines. Crows were screaming at the tops of their lungs, filling the hollow with harsh, drawn-out caws. I crouched in a patch of brush and waited. Wingbeats of incoming crows cleft the air. The black horde swarmed around a pine in a clearing. Crows dashed in and out of the tree, screeching at something inside.

As the crescendo mounted, an owl flushed from the evergreen. On broad wings it flew through the trees, the crows slashing close. One crow bored in and raked the owl's back with its feet; another pecked its skull. As the owl half-rolled to confront his attackers, his wing struck a branch and he fell. He hit ground thirty feet from where I sat.

Crows landed in trees all around. The owl rolled onto his back, beak chattering, talons poised. The crows castigated him like a hundred black-robed revivalists confronting Beelzebub. Caught in the middle of this unbridled hatred, I felt the hair rise on the back of my neck and prayed the flock would not notice me. Finally the owl righted himself with slow dignity, looked about, and fled. The crows followed, taking their din over the ridge.

I walked softly the rest of that day, and sudden shadows made me flinch.

Crows. Common black birds, components of the landscape, canny survivors tempting us to throw anthropomorphic words their way: raffish, brazen, insolent, devious, irreverent. Crows have managed to alienate humankind to a degree achieved by few other animals. Crows seem to laugh off the danger inherent in such bad blood, bend under the accompanying persecution, and prosper despite it.

Take a close look at Crow. The first thing you will note about him is his color—coal black from bill to tail-tip. It's as if he decided a long time ago that suiting up in colorful or cryptic garb was a waste of time better spent snooping about for a free feed. Crow can afford to be an exclamation point against his surroundings because of his size and aggressiveness, his catholic eating habits, and his social lifestyle.

Look at Crow's beak. It has not yet decided if it wants to be a hammer, a probe, a hook, or a dagger. It works quite well as each. Under the skin, it connects to a complex system of hinges and levers that lets the upper bill move simultaneously with the lower when the beak is opening. With such a maw, Crow can swallow large items with ease.

Or he can pick them up in his sharp-clawed feet. Crow does dexterous things with his feet—filches nestlings, carries off corn, even dips into schools of fish to grab a meal—things other perching birds have not yet thought to do.

Now take Crow by his feet, invert him, and shake. He will squall, not to elicit pity but to summon help. Any crows within hearing will come without hesitation, spoiling for a fight. (A chink in Crow's armor, as we will note later.) At this time you will release Crow to his friends or risk a mobbing. Being mobbed is no fun at all, whether you are owl, fox, cat, or human, and a mobbing may become more than a scolding. Nature writer John Madson relates that a friend trying to dispatch a wounded crow was mobbed by a flock that cut him about the face before driving him to cover in a willow thicket.

The crow's taxonomic name is *Corvus brachyrynchos*, which sounds like ancient profanity but in fact means "short-beaked Corvid." The crow belongs to Family Corvidae, a clan embracing all manner of scalawags: ravens, jays, magpies, and Clark's nut-

134

cracker in North America, jackdaws, choughs, and rooks in the Old World. Corvids have the largest cerebrums, relative to body size, of all birds, and scientists believe them to be the smartest. Among the Corvids, the crow sits near the front of the class.

One index of intelligence is language, and crows have an intricate one well suited to a social existence. Using its seven pairs of syringeal muscles, a crow can manipulate the pitch and rate of its calling to announce its presence to other crows; threaten fellows for food or roosting spots; upbraid a predator; rally its colleagues to harass the predator; or sound retreat. In all, twenty-three separate vocalizations have been described. First-rate mimics, crows embellish their vocabularies with various kinds of sounds: steam whistles, whining dogs, a hen squawking, a rooster crowing, a child crying. Captive crows learn to imitate human speech and laughter (probably the derisive brand).

The wider a crow travels, the more likely he'll understand his Corvid relatives' dialects. Captive Pennsylvania crows do not respond normally to distress or assembly cries of Maine crows, and vice versa. (To the Pennsylvanians' credit, a Down East accent *is* rather hard to understand.) More cosmopolitan crows breeding in Pennsylvania and wintering in the South among fish crows respond to the distress call of the French jackdaw, a cousin they have never met, while untraveled American crows do not react to the Gallic bird's cry.

Crows are survivors. To and from work, I travel a long stretch of country road where I see dead foxes, raccoons, cats, and deer—supposedly smart creatures—and a host of lesser beasts. I see plenty of crows pecking at the dead. They flap up just high enough to let my truck roll past, then fall back to gleaning calories from the gore. Never have I seen a road-killed crow.

As social birds, crows gain several advantages. Their numbers distract predators, which find it hard to zero in on a single bird. Crows can drive predators away by force of numbers. In a group, the individual crow can devote more time to feeding or resting, because more sets of senses are periodically checking up on the environment. (Crows so occupied also post sentries in nearby trees to watch for danger. If a predator kills a crow, says a persistent folk belief, the rest of the flock will try a negligent sentry—and sometimes execute him.)

Crows can tell an unarmed man from a man with a gun. They can count. If three gunners walk into a copse of trees and only two come out, the crows will know something's up. Crows drop clams and walnuts on highways to be crushed by cars. One Scandinavian crow even learned to ice fish: He would wait for a fisherman's tip-up flag to signal a catch, then grab the line in his beak and tug it in, clamping it down with his feet to keep it from slipping back, finally dragging the fish onto the ice and eating all but the hook.

Crows' eating habits probably got them in trouble with men in the first place. Accomplished generalists, they devour corn, oats, sorghum, wheat, grapes, cherries, cranberries, strawberries, garden vegetables, dogfood straight out of the dish, worms, insects, the eggs and young of other birds, carrion . . . and so on.

Although crows have often been condemned for depleting cornfields, a study in five New York counties indicated that corn made up less than 14 percent of the birds' annual diet, with most of that taken in winter. In May, when farmers sow corn in central New York, it came to 1 percent. To make the situation more ambiguous, one biologist estimates that a single family of crows—two adults and four or five young—consumes some forty thousand grubs, caterpillars, army worms, and other injurious insects during the nesting season alone.

Hunters have long begrudged crows their annual take of eggs and nestlings. On one marsh, only four ducklings hatched from two hundred eggs; crows pilfered the rest. In Canada, a study of five hundred nests found that half were destroyed before hatching, with crows wrecking 31 percent. While researching the blue-winged teal during the 1930s, Dr. Logan Bennett found "pecks of crow-destroyed [duck] eggs" around Iowa marshes, but felt that almost all had been promiscuously laid before serious nesting had begun, and thus would not have hatched. Certainly nest predation

136

forces many ducks, pheasants, and grouse to renest each spring. But several rounds of nesting make it less likely that bad weather will destroy a high percentage of a year's hatch.

Crows do a lot of eating, but they get eaten, too. Primary eater is the great horned owl, whose range coincides with the crow's across the continent. To Crow, Owl is chief terror and nightmare, the thing that goes bump in the night. Owl likes to slip into a crow roost on silent wings, strike repeatedly, and feast on heads and brains.

Crow remembers Owl's transgressions all the days of his life. The hoots of an owl prompt intense and rapid scolding from any crow within hearing. Should a crow spot an owl in its daytime hideout, the black bird will sound assembly, tolling in relatives from near and far. Although a band of crows could certainly kill an owl, there's no indication they ever do. They get close, maybe pull a few feathers, but, being survivors at heart, content themselves with delivering vocal abuse.

This deep hatred has not gone unnoticed by man. If a gunner hangs an owl decoy in a tree—a stuffed bird or even a plastic replica—and mimics the crow assembly cry using either a mouth call or a tape recording, he can draw crows to ambush. Whipped to a frenzy, the birds ignore shotgun blasts and may be killed by the hundreds.

While such gunning makes no real dent in the crow population, attacking a roost may. Crows sleep in groups at night, usually in dense vegetation offering protection from heavy weather. Roosts can be huge, especially in winter. In the late 1800s, up to two hundred thousand crows occupied twenty acres in Arlington National Cemetery; a twenty-acre grove in Montgomery County, Pennsylvania, has harbored at least that many; and in central Kansas, a big catalpa stand is said to shelter ten million.

During the 1920s and 1930s, roosts were sometimes bombed in an effort to reduce crop damage. Near Harrisburg, Illinois, locals infiltrated a roost one day when the crows were out feeding, and festooned the trees with a thousand steel tubes filled with dynamite. Detonated after the crows returned, the bombs killed a hundred thousand.

Roost bombing is a thing of the past. If local populations appear thinner this decade than last, look to habitat: roosting sites swallowed by housing, brushy feeding grounds converted to cropland, wooded nesting areas lumbered off. The national population, however, doesn't seem to be hurting; the U.S. Fish and Wildlife Service reported no significant change in the country's crow population from 1966 to 1974.

In 1972, bureaucracy gave the crow a helping hand. When the United States and Mexico amended their migratory bird treaty that year, Mexico insisted on including Corvidae in an effort to protect certain jays. Crows, of course, are part of the family. Now federal law restricts crow hunting to 124 days a year, with the states allowed to set season dates, bag limits, shooting hours, and the like, providing that crows may not be taken during their peak nesting period. There's a Catch 22 from the crows' viewpoint, though: "A Federal permit shall not be required to control crows when [they are] committing or about to commit depredations upon ornamental or shade trees, agricultural crops, livestock or wildlife."

Depredations. A lovely word describing so many crow activities. Crow is probably smirking at his sudden registry within the law—and his just-as-sudden eviction.

Not long after I watched the crows mob the owl, I saw another fight involving a crow. This time Crow was on the receiving end, as two kingbirds routed him from a patch of brush. More maneuverable than their larger foe, the kingbirds darted in and pecked Crow's back. Crow squawked sullenly and beat it for open fields, where he gained altitude and finally left his pursuers behind.

It felt good to see a crow so discomfited, and I laughed out loud. Likely the black brigand had been trying to rob the kingbirds' nest and had gotten what he deserved.

I looked for the nest. There it was, a shaggy cup filling the fork of a hawthorn. Four eggs inside.

Bzipp! I ducked and looked around. From my blind side the second kingbird ripped air an inch above my head. The birds chattered with rage. Bent low, I hustled out of the patch. A crow without wings, I beat my retreat as best I could.

Stoltzfus Consignment Sale

"You should dress well," Jeff Swabb said. He studied my muddy boots, frayed work pants, and denim jacket, shook his head, and looked back out the truck window. "You should look like you're there to buy. Bid without hesitating. And never stop on a round number. The other guy may have decided to go fifty bucks, or seventy-five, or a hundred. You'll be surprised what you can get for an extra five."

We drove down the long valley. On either side of the road, tan fields stretched away to gray-purple hills, dotted with green hemlocks. In a woodlot, buckets hung from spiles bored into maple trees. A farmer, getting an early start on the year, plowed a field; seagulls pecked in his wake.

We passed a flat, horse-drawn wagon with two riders sitting on a bale of straw. Their wide-brimmed black hats glinted in the sun. Where a dirt road joined the main, a van waited. In it were eight men wearing black porkpie hats. The van turned onto the blacktop behind us. Ahead, an Amish man was hiking along the berm; a pickup truck stopped, the man climbed in back, and the truck lurched into motion again.

It looked like everyone in Brush Valley would be at the Stoltzfus Consignment Sale.

We had to walk the last quarter-mile. Trucks lined the road, battered Chevy pickups, Broncos with balloon tires, and four-wheel-drive Ramchargers whose side mirrors stood higher than my head. A fleet of black buggies occupied a field, their singletrees down in the mud.

The crowd looked like a mixed flock of birds—mostly crows, with orioles, cardinals, thrashers, and jays.

People stood in knots around the auctioneers, whose voices rang off the gray weathered walls of Stoltzfus's barn. Amish women wearing gold-framed glasses herded little girls in bonnets. Young men lounged on truck bumpers. Big-bellied men stood talking, hands in pockets, boot toes tracing patterns in the dirt. Three boys in black hats surveyed the scene from atop a milking shed; pigeons, temporarily displaced, circled against the deep blue sky.

Jeff and I ran into Walter Barger, a farmer-welder who earns considerable income unfreezing water pipes. This winter the freeze-ups had begun early and ended late—Walter told us he thawed his last line on March 3, some three weeks ago—and were exacerbated by drought, which prevented people from running their water to keep it from freezing.

Walter had paid me a visit the day after Christmas. The temperature stood at ten degrees when he drove his truck into the yard, clumped into the house, and hooked a pair of cables from his arc welder onto my water line. Electricity coursed through the cables, generated by a big engine on the back of the truck. The current heated the pipe, melting the ice. He charged twenty-five dollars.

"I had to unfreeze one woman four times this year," Walter said. "Another welder, he did it at least that many. Makes an expensive winter, so it does."

Walter admitted to thawing his own pipes twice.

A wind whipped through the barnyard, whirling dust and corn husks in the air. The children at the sale—all looked to be Amish—ran past the men's legs, pelted each other with clods, and hid behind their mothers' skirts. It was a Thursday, but apparently the valley's one-room schools had closed for the event.

Jeff was hailed by a man wearing an orange sweatshirt and a red baseball cap. Jeff is a gunsmith, and a fine one, and he is apt to be cornered at any rural gathering. Red Baseball Cap wanted him to install an adjustable trigger on his favorite deer rifle, and to glass-bed two or three other guns. They settled down to business, and I wandered off.

Beside Stoltzfus's big white house stood a garage. Four lines of people fed into the open bays. I stood in one line to pick up a bidding number. Another line led me to two whoopie pies, a carton of milk, and a slab of cherry pie—a hard choice among the pumpkin, shoofly, blueberry, and peach.

Outside, I watched the auctioneers while I ate.

One was selling bolts of cloth, pillows, and curtain material. Women fingered the fabric. The auctioneer's client, a swarthy man with red-dyed hair, waved the goods in the air and proclaimed their value in thickly accented English. He berated the auctioneer for letting them go too cheaply.

A second auctioneer sold food—cannisters of potato chips, boxes of cookies, cartons of candy—and tools. He worked for a wiry, gray-bearded Amish entrepreneur, who stood in a wagon and passed down items for the bidding. The auctioneer sold a hammer, a digging bar, a staple gun, and a leather apron. When bidding on a tool chest began to lag, the Amish man broke in, saying he needed twenty for the chest and would not let it go for a penny less. Yelled a man from the crowd, "You can get one for fifteen at the K-Mart." The bidders hooted, and the Amish man glared and jerked the chest back.

The auctioneers' staccato voices competed with each other. The tool peddler threw a package of cheese crackers at the dry goods auctioneer, narrowly missing. "Shut up, you!" he screeched.

I ran into Carolyn Petrus, a raven-haired woman in her early thirties, who makes her living buying and selling antique quilts. She goes to a lot of auctions. She told me how to signal a half-bid: with one hand, strike the opposite forearm to offer the auctioneer one-half the increment he seeks.

Carolyn pointed out members of different Amish sects, including several from Kishacoquillas Valley, fifteen miles to the south in neighboring Mifflin County. The women wore different styles of bonnets and aprons, the men different hats. Some of the groups drove distinctive styles of carriages, Carolyn said. I wondered how early they had gotten up in the morning to drive their buggies over the mountain.

I left Carolyn and picked my way across the barnyard. A third auctioneer, a lean, dark-featured man, held forth on a bank beside the barn. He brandished a cane at a horse collar held aloft by an Amish youth. The cane swung toward the crowd. The auctioneer orchestrated the bidding, pointing right, left, at a man in back, his voice building to a crescendo that fell abruptly to the word "sold."

Harnesses, wagon tongues, welding rods, burlap bags, nails. The bidders were all men. I stood next to a young Amish man with piercing blue eyes, his neck deeply nicked from a fresh shave. He bid tentatively, and lost out on a bale of wire.

I felt a touch at my elbow. "Buy anything yet?" Jeff asked.

"No. Let's go look at what else they're going to sell."

In a pasture north of the barn sat farm machinery—harrows, rakes, drills, balers, green and red and yellow, some rusty and dented, some shining clean. Off to the side we found milk cans, crates, lumber, plywood, animal cages, washing machines, a lathe, stoves, doors, locust fenceposts, a bed, and an ancient red bulldozer with a green easy chair bolted where the seat should have been. "I've always wanted a bulldozer," said Jeff. Why? "Keep the lane level, snake logs out of the woods, chase the dogs around."

Jeff agreed not to wait for the auctioneer. "Afraid you might actually buy the thing?" I asked.

We drifted through Stoltzfus's barn between rows of black-and-white cows. In back of the stalls, a half-dozen boys talked in low tones; three girls in white bonnets were just leaving. In a shed behind the barn stood a team of mules, long-eared, lantern-jawed beasts with roached manes. One mule reared on his front hooves and kicked his neighbor lightly in the ribs with his rear hooves. He kicked four times, his hooves returning to the ground after each

blow—*whump-clop, whump-clop, whump-clop, whump-clop*.
Warnings, or maybe just muleplay. The kicker looked back over
his shoulder. The kicked mule blinked.

In the lee of the barn, a game was in progress. A crowd of men
and boys sat and stood watching. At the center of the action, a
square of cornstalks blanketed the ground. On each of the four
sides around the stalks lay a fence rail, perhaps fifty feet away from
the rail on the opposite side.

Behind each rail stood an Amish or a Mennonite youth. In the
center, two other boys crouched on the cornstalks. One of the boys
on the perimeter fired a ball at a boy in the middle—his target
leaped aside and the ball sailed far out in the yard, landing amid
dung and mud. The spectators laughed and called out as the boy
who had missed walked off to the sidelines.

Three players remained on the perimeter. They sailed the ball
around the ring to each other. The ball slapped their hands. They
faked throws at the dodgers in the middle; they changed posi-
tions, darting from one rail to the next, three boys for the four
places. The dodgers eyed them warily, weaving and shuffling like
boxers, always leaping around to face the ball.

An errant throw landed nearby, and I tossed it back. The ball
was a little smaller than a baseball, as hard as a softball, with a
cover of loose, red leather.

The ball darted hand-to-hand around the ring. Finally a
thrower sailed it over the heads of the dodgers to a partner who
had snuck in on the other side. A quick peg by the second thrower
struck one of the dodgers flush on the backside. The crowd roared.
The stricken youth got up, brushed himself off, and left the game.
Soon a second thrower missed and went out, leaving just two.
They finally banished the remaining dodger, who was struck on
the boot as he tried to leap over a hot throw.

New players filled the ranks as the game progressed. A lanky
Mennonite, hat adorned with a blue feather, dodged for a full five
minutes before the ball struck him on the elbow and caromed off
across the yard. An Amish youth with wide eyes and unruly hair

144

hurled with authority and caught the ball one-handed. His quick release sent dodger after dodger out of the ring. An old man came to watch, and the boys called him to play; he grinned and waved them away, and sat by the barn on a hay bale, his back against the sunny boards.

When Jeff and I returned to the sale, we found the crowd as thick as when we had arrived. I asked a fellow where Melvin Stoltzfus, the owner of the farm, might be found. He pointed out an Amish man of medium height wearing black trousers, suspenders, and a shirt with the sleeves rolled up.

Stoltzfus gave my hand a firm shake. He told me he believed seven or eight hundred people had come to the sale. The event was in its ninth year, and it had grown "almost too big." I asked him why he held it. One reason, of course, was that he received a commission on everything sold. Also, "I just like auctions." Last year the sale was earlier in March—wet and muddy. This year? He smiled, lifting his face to the cloudless sky.

A gaunt, bearded man came up and spoke to Stoltzfus in Pennsylvania Dutch, a deep stutter marring his speech. Stoltzfus nodded and replied. He shot me a grin and was off, calling over his shoulder, "Stop by sometime and we'll visit."

Jeff and I made one last circuit of the sale. Neither of us had bid on anything, and there was nothing left that we wanted. We didn't mind. It had been enough to feel the strengthening sun and to shake off the drowsy winter feeling—we'd gotten the stink blown off, as the Dutch say.

We walked down Stoltzfus's lane, behind a man carrying a door on his back.

The Perfect Hat

My cousin Jack, who lived in Cody, Wyoming, used to wear a purple cowboy hat to the rodeo in Meeteetse. He wore it to elicit insults which he could turn into invitations to fight. I have a mental image of Jack touching his fingertips to the hat's brim, lifting it lightly off his sunburned head, handing it to a friend, and swarming all over his opponent. Jack weighed 145 pounds and had been an all-state tackle in football.

I don't know where the purple cowboy hat got to. Jack got to British Columbia, where he met his match in a woman. Here in Pennsylvania I see plenty of cowboy hats these days, none purple and most of them on the heads of truck drivers and auctioneers and people who own riding horses. I wonder if they still wear them out West.

There's something about a hat. A good hat warms your head or keeps it cool, directs the rain away from your neck, shields your eyes from the sun—and more. I once heard a saying that a man wearing a hat is an unknown quantity, although perhaps that depends on the hat.

These days, hats are in style. The Eddie Bauer people—they will mail you a color catalog full of fastidious models attired in Classic Raglan Jackets and Blizzard Master Vests and Mt. Everest Underwear—market a wide line of hats, all fashionably, steeply priced. There is the Yakima ($65), heavy felt with a leather sweatband, shaped to what the catalog calls "subtle Western styling"—sort of a wishy-washy cowboy hat. They offer the Derringer ("a favorite of ranchers and executives alike"); the Safari Hat ("wide snap brim fends off blazing sun"); and the Greek Fisherman's Cap, whose "Mediterranean flair" would undoubtedly have served Cousin Jack as effectively as the color of his Stetson. Two new offerings from Bauer are the Wildcatter and the Fortune Hunter, $110 the pair. Both are fedoras, with broad brims snapped down front and back. Tough-guy, movie-star hats. Walter Mitty hats.

I don't look particularly good in a hat. I often wear eyeglasses and I have a size seven-and-three-eighths head, so a hat usually makes me look too cluttered upstairs, or top-heavy. Even so, I have felt compelled to buy a wide range of hats over the years. Some perform specific outdoor functions. Several I have never worn, except in front of a mirror. Quite a few have become separated from me. It is a strange truth that hats are almost never thrown away: They just turn up missing.

I can recall at least twenty hats. The following is an incomplete and unchronological listing.

"Goose Down Sportsman's Cap." Bought through the mail from Eddie Bauer, this is a warm and useful piece of clothing. Its ear flaps may be turned down and tied under the chin (not suggested when hunting deer, because you can't hear), or tied over the crown. Its visor, long like a baseball cap's, keeps snow off the eyeglasses. It looks like the hat worn by Elmer Fudd. It is brilliant orange.

"Moose River Hat." Another mail-order, this one from L. L. Bean. While my atlas lists Moose Creeks, Hills, Heights, Islands, Jaws, Passes, Mountains, and Lakes, I find no Moose River. Maybe it's in Maine, where Bean's is located. Anyway, the hat is a beauty, one of the few I own that looks good on me. (Personal opinion.) It is a fedora, pale gray, with a hatband fashioned from a rattlesnake skin. (I didn't kill the snake, but could not pass up the offer of its hide.) As are all broad-brimmed hats, the Moose River is good for wearing on a walk, no good for hunting: Every blackberry cane, every hawthorn branch, stands ready to knock it off.

"British Felt Hat." Another fedora, dark green, also from Bean's. I treated myself to it before leaving on a backpacking trip in the Rockies. When the hat arrived, I unpacked it and passed it back and forth through the steam of a teakettle until it went limp; then I pressed a furrow into the crown, snapped the front brim to a jaunty angle, and stuck the hat in the freezer to set. In the mountains the hat performed admirably, until it snowed. The morning after the storm, the temperature huddled in the twenties and a wind whipped grains of ice across the high meadows. My two companions jammed their motley Stetsons into their packs and brought out stocking caps of wool. I had a stocking cap in my pack, but couldn't bear to crumple my fedora. I endured cold ears to preserve a Gary Cooper crease.

On the next trip, I wised up. I took an old Stetson and trimmed the brim with tin snips—to keep my pack from jamming it from behind—and crushed and crumpled to my heart's content.

I had bought the Stetson about ten years before. The purchase was an awkward business. As in buying any hat, I was forced to try it on before the cynical eye of a salesman who of course lied and told me how good I looked—a virtual impossibility in an immaculate, characterless headpiece. The transaction took place in a Western clothing store in Cody. As I tried on the full range of Stetsons—gray ones, black, brown, tan, high-crowned, flat-brimmed—I felt like the rankest of tourists on his way to Yellowstone Park. At the time I was working on a ranch nearby, and I consoled myself with the notion that the clerk, a tired-looking man in a plaid shirt and string tie, might see me later when some of the sheen had worn off.

The rancher I was staying with had a marvelous Stetson. The hat was of indeterminate age and gray as a mule deer's belly. Its brim, paper-thin and ripply, was tugged down in front—"bulldogged," in the local parlance—to give the hat a scimitar shape from the side. The man wore it year-round. In winter he wore it over a section of woman's hose, which snugged his ears to his skull to keep them warm.

My warmest hat is a tightly woven stocking cap, the kind the farmers wear in Switzerland; like the rancher's improvisation, it tucks my ears against my head and comes down nearly to my eyebrows. It is brown wool, and dangling from the top is a string of yarn with a bulbous, fringed end, resembling a cow's tail. It is almost as exotic and somewhat less bizarre than the Peruvian mountain hats that are occasionally seen, particolored caps that cling to the head like wilted flying helmets.

Another warm hat I own is a so-called "Chicom hat," short for Chinese communist hat, a black leather affair with three flaps (one in front and one on each side) that sits on top of the head like a pillbox. I have a Balaclava helmet: a wool watch cap that unfolds to cover neck, throat, and chin, with a slit to see through. I wear it rarely because it scratches, but it is a traditional mountaineering design and I think I'd better hang on to it.

In summer, hats minimize glare and sunburn. There is no evidence that they stave off heat stroke or heat exhaustion. The brain will not bake without heat protection; in fact, a hat must be ventilated or it will make your head hotter.

My favorite summer hat is a wide-brimmed straw hat of the type commonly worn by Amish men; despite its nineteenth-century design, it remains state-of-the-art summer headwear, allowing zephyrs to penetrate its weave and keeping gnats at a distance. I had for a while a white terry-cloth slouch hat that could be soaked in water before wearing to keep the head cool. I dyed it green to make it less obtrusive in the woods; for a long time after, every time I wore it, the upper half of my forehead turned green.

Baseball caps have been the rage the last few summers. Not caps bearing names of major league teams, but caps advertising every corporation, conglomerate, and consortium imaginable, from symphony orchestras to embalming fluid suppliers. My immediate family owns six: Dekalb Corn; Wampler Foods; Beech-Nut Chewing Tobacco; Wayne Animal Health Aids; CAT Diesel Power (my wife's cap; it bears, not inappropriately, the gold braid of admiralty on its brim); and Worley Okay Feed Mills of Clovis,

New Mexico (alternating panels of yellow, royal blue, and scarlet, an improbably high crown, and a little blue button on the summit).

One of my best hats is a rain hat, a true sou'wester, a backwards-looking contraption that is standard wear for blue-water sailors and lobster fishermen. It is black and sinister, the rubber smudged gray like an old inner tube. It has ear flaps and an elongated back brim that fairly spouts water in a storm. I have used it on rainy day deer stands, and it really works.

My favorite hat, however, is the cheapest hat I own. It is a Jones cap, a design that features a rounded crown and a narrow brim that can be worn folded up or turned down. This particular cap is camouflaged with blotches of brown and green; the inside lining bears a repeating print of a stick-figure hunter following a dysplastic setter. Locally, this type of headgear is called a "hooftie hat." It provides excellent camouflage in morel covers, filling stations, and taverns.

These, then, are my hats. I own others considerably more embarrassing, and refuse to describe them here. I would like to state categorically, however, that I do not own a Tyrolean hat (with or without a tassel of boar bristles that could double as a shaving brush); a pith helmet; a French beret; a swordfisherman's cap (a cloth cap with a black bill so hugely long and tapering that it makes the wearer look like a stork); a straw boater; or anything else so ridiculous.

There is, however, one hat I must add to my collection, the perfect country man's hat. The writer T. H. White told me about it in his journal, *England Have My Bones*.

"Among other lessons which I have learnt in Scotland," White wrote, "there is the fact that only one hat at present manufactured by the human race is of any use at all . . . and this is the deerstalker or twa-snooted bonnet. If you fish in a blizzard for a fortnight, you learn that the back of your neck is more important than your forehead. If you fish in a cap you find that, after a certain pitch of misery has been passed, the cap gets turned back to front.

It is better to have a wet face than a wet back. The twa-snooted bonnet protects both quarters, besides having two admirable flaps with which it is possible to comfort the ears in a snowstorm.'' White wore his twa-snooted in the game covers, where a gunning partner, an English farmer, commented on its strategic possibilities. ''You'll be able to circumvent them today,'' he said. ''They won't know whether you're coming or going.''

A Small Brown Package

In the bogs and thickets near my home there lives a retiring bird of outlandish appearance and singular habit. Its large eyes crowd the top and back of its head; its ears are forward of its eyes; and its bill looks far too long for its body. In earliest spring, the male flies through the chill, twilight skies, singing to attract a mate. The hen broods a clutch of eggs though late snow may cover her. And the chicks—bundles of camouflaged fuzz—begin to fly when but a fortnight old.

The bird is the American woodcock, a prime example of nature's wont to conceal, in a small brown package, life both complex and beautiful.

The woodcock is a portly, quail-size bird. Its legs are stubby, its wings short and rounded to permit flight among trees. Taxonomists place it with the shorebirds, and indeed there are shared characteristics, but the link seems odd: Shorebirds are owned by wind and sun and broad, sandy strands, while the woodcock is a creature of damp cow pastures and brush-crowded creeks.

In March, after wintering farther south, woodcock return to their boggy haunts in Pennsylvania and other points north. Directly they set about mating, and now they are most easily observed, especially the males, who choose singing grounds—open patches in dense groundcover—for their eloquent dawn-and-dusk ritual.

Each March I try to spend an evening or two on a local singing ground. I show up just before dark, when woodcock activity is triggered by light of the proper intensity—0.05 foot-candles, to be exact, a level at which binoculars become particularly useless and one sees more clearly by looking near objects rather than straight at them.

A male woodcock announces his act by sounding a single note, represented most often as *peent*. The note has an insect-like timbre suggesting the rasp of the nighthawk, that sound of summer that resonates from graveled city roofs. After a quarter-hour and a hundred or so *peents*, the woodcock flits up on whistling wings. In a series of wide spirals he climbs a hundred yards, poises against the sky, and slips toward earth. Like a leaf he falls, warbling a song described as *p chuck tuck cuck oo*, a liquid melody hard to pinpoint and sometimes seeming to come from several birds at once. When the woodcock touches down—softly, like a dropped rag—he sounds that nasal *peent*.

Activity peaks on clear, windless evenings, and on moonlit nights the birds carry on well past dark. The show, of course, is to impress females, despite the fact that there may be none within miles; males often return north ahead of their potential mates, and many early performances are given in vain.

I like to steal onto a singing ground when the woodcock is in the air. I lie on my belly in the cold, wet grass, craning my neck to watch the bird drift down. Often he lands within a few feet, and I note that his predictable *peent* follows a soft, gurgling *tuko*. He does a turkey strut, short tail fanned like an aspen leaf, wings touching the ground, bill held high. Sometimes he trips in the grass.

Either the courtship flight's charm is not widely known, or most people see little point in spending a cold March evening watching a bird fly up and down: I rarely encounter anyone on a singing ground. Once a friend met two wildlife biology students who complained about not having enough light to film the flights. The students thought that outfitting a male woodcock with a pair of dark contact lenses might trick him into flying an hour earlier, when they could make pictures. We never learned if they managed to do this.

A cock persists in his flights for weeks on end. If his routine strikes a hen's fancy, mating takes place. Afterward, the female quits the field and does not associate with the male again. Later she moves to suitable nesting cover, usually within a few hundred yards of the singing ground. The hen prepares to raise a brood, and the cock gets on with the day-to-day business of resting and feeding.

Woodcock do most of their foraging at night, probing their out-size bills into soft earth to locate worms, their principal food. Sensitive tactile corpuscles at the end of the beak detect the underground prey, and a special bone-muscle arrangement lets a bird open only the very tip of its bill, clamp down on a victim, and pull it from the soil.

Apparently its penchant for worms helped shape the woodcock's form. Sometime after the species left the shore for the uplands, its eyes moved to the back of the skull to let the probing bird watch for trouble from behind. (Today's woodcock sees better to the rear than ahead, perhaps explaining its tendency to fly into branches.) As the eyes retreated, the ears were forced into the gap between the eyesockets and the bill. And, in an obvious adaptation for probing, the nostrils climbed to the base of the lengthening bill. All of this cranial shifting set the brain in motion, too. The forebrain got shoved back, and the mid-brain and hind-brain rotated down and slightly forward. The woodcock's cerebellum—controlling body movement and balance—came to lie below the rest of the brain and above the spinal column, instead of occupying the rear of the skull, as it does in other birds. The woodcock of today has an upside-down brain.

This pattern of evolution is unsubstantiated by fossil record. It is also moot, since we don't understand the twentieth-century woodcock very well. Much of the problem lies in the bird's nocturnal lifestyle and overgrown habitat. As ornithologist Arthur C. Bent wrote, "Its quiet, retiring habits do not lead to human intimacy."

154

Confusion reigns on several fronts. We do not know, for example, whether a male occupies the same singing ground throughout the breeding season. Nor are we sure that he is promiscuous; when one early naturalist collected a female, her young were then reared by another bird—presumably her mate. Controversy also centers on the female carrying a newly hatched chick between her legs when she is flushed from the nest. A respected ornithology text says she does, the most exhaustive woodcock book says she doesn't—except perhaps by accident.

Until recently, woodcock enthusiasts argued about the twittering the bird makes when taking off: Is it vocal, or mechanical? It fell to biologist William Sheldon to snip the three stiff, narrow, outer primaries from the wings of a singing male. The bird continued to fly and sing, but twittered no more.

Not open to debate is the woodcock's superlative protective coloring. The feathers—each a mosaic of brown, cinnamon, tan, black—form irregular patches of eye-catching colors that draw attention away from the shape of the bird itself.

The woodcock hen is famous for sitting tight on her eggs, relying instinctively on her cryptic garb. Sheldon noted that discovering an incubating hen is "largely a matter of chance, even when crews of assistants are available for a systematic search." Wrote English zoologist H. B. Cott, "Standing in the open and moving cautiously, but freely, I have photographed a nesting Woodcock which was so confident that she suffered me to place one leg of the tripod within a few inches of her body, and to remove with my hand unsightly grasses from her very nest."

The chicks—almost always four per brood—are likewise well-camouflaged. In hand, they appear brightly marked with their dark-brown-on-buff stripes, yet against a background of leaves, twigs, and stems, they almost disappear. Chicks leave the nest a few hours after hatching; the hen feeds them for several days, but then they are probing on their own. Development is swift; after two weeks they can fly short distances, and in two more weeks they resemble adults.

Woodcock migrate, although not on the far-flung scale of their shorebird cousins. Autumn's freezing nights start them south. Wrote John James Audubon: ". . . these birds, although they migrate singly, follow each other with such rapidity, that they may be said to arrive in flocks, the one coming directly in the wake of the other." Eventually, most woodcock arrive in the South, concentrating along the Gulf Coast in Louisiana and Mississippi.

Woodcock travel by night. Their pace is leisurely, ten to ninety or more miles a night interspersed by days spent feeding and resting. The loose flocks, called flights, may crowd suitable covers with scores of birds, a phenomenon occupying an almost mythic position in upland bird hunting. The literature of this sport is replete with references to flight birds, to muddy, spirited English setters (ever loath to flush, woodcock permit classic dog work and close gunning), to telltale chalky droppings on dank ground, to yellow-gold aspens, to simple, pleasant days afield.

Mr. Detwiler

When I first saw him, I tried to duck back into the pines, but he raised his hand in greeting and I was stuck. All the while he was coming on over through the hawthorns, I cussed under my breath. It was bad enough finding a stranger in my favorite bird cover, but it would be even worse if I had to jaw with him as the afternoon slipped away.

When he got near, he whistled in his dog, a gaunt setter marked with a black saddle and brown spots above her eyes. The dog had that slight jerkiness of gait that suggests age; so did her master.

"Hello," he said, clicking open his shotgun and crooking the barrels over his arm. "Name's Detwiler. And you'd be . . .?"

"Fergus. Chuck Fergus."

He stretched out a hand, and I shook it. A rough hand, bigger than mine, though its owner stood inches shorter.

"D'you hunt around here much?" he asked.

"Some."

"Seen many birds today?"

"No," I lied. "This cover's only so-so."

He grinned, and I knew he'd taken in the one-grouse bulge in my game pouch.

"Have you hunted this valley before?" I asked.

He nodded. "Used to quite a bit, years ago."

"How was the hunting then?"

He smiled, lines around his eyes sort of falling into place, and reached down to scratch behind his dog's ears. "It was good," he said. "Wasn't it, Kate?"

He dug in his pocket for a chaw, and I knew I was caught.

As he filled his cheek, I looked him over. His coat was canvas, brush-frazzled and dotted with stick-tights and beggar's-lice. Canvas pants and boots—those sixteen-inchers you see in old pictures, the kind that make even the stockiest legs look spindly—with gray wool socks folded down over the tops. On his head perched a black-and-red-checked cap, brim broken in the middle; below the cap brown eyes shone in a weathered face that could have been sixty years old, or eighty.

I realized he was holding out the tobacco pouch—"Mechanic's Delight"—and shook my head.

"Fergus," he said, cocking his head. "I know the name from somewhere."

I groaned inwardly. Sometimes, in filling stations, gun shops, country stores, taverns, I hear this preface followed by an identification as "the fella who writes for the 'Game News,'" and then I can expect a rambling treatise on why there aren't any rabbits, why the deer population's shot to heck, and, in the next breath, the twenty-seven bucks the discourser killed off the same stand in twenty-seven years of hunting.

"Don't you write for that little magazine . . .?"

I nodded, resigning myself to an afternoon shot, to grouse and woodcock unbagged, and to an inescapable ensnarement rivaled only by childhood memories of Saturdays when my parents, too smart to leave me to my own devices, dragged me from store to store while they shopped for furniture.

But the old man only smiled and let his eyes wander over the hunting cover. At length he turned. "Whyn't we hunt together?" he said. "Kate's pretty fair on birds, and I see you haven't got a dog."

"All right." I felt relieved; hunting with the old man—however slow he might be—seemed infinitely better than standing around talking.

When the old fellow shut his smoothbore, I noticed the gun for the first time. A standard American double, with a straight-backed setter engraved on the lockplates. The barrel ends were brush-whipped a fine silver-gray, and the stock was nicked. A sturdy, utilitarian shotgun that looked just right in those briar-scratched hands. I supposed the old gent had got it when you could still buy a well-made piece of shooting hardware—with enough fancy to make it special—for something less than an arm and a leg.

He noticed my gaze. "My new gun," he said, turning it in his hands. "Shoots all right, and it's got the new steel barrels. But it ain't the same as my old Winchester." He flicked the double to his shoulder. "No, sir. When you looked between hammers as many times as I did, it's hard getting used to a hammerless."

He stopped short and watched me out of the corner of his eye. Then he turned abruptly and whistled. "Kate! Birds—go get 'em."

The dog leaped away. She wore a bell, and its tinkle carried clearly through the late-afternoon air. The old man nodded, and we followed her into the goldenrod and thornapples.

The setter was a close worker, and I saw her strike her first bird. She stopped at the scent, turned, and crept to the edge of a fallen apple tree bristling with shoots. She stood high-stationed, tail straight out, like the setter on the old man's gun.

We went in, and a grouse burst from the rear of the thicket, straight away and low, anybody's bird. I got on it fast, but by the time my safety was off, feathers were adrift and the echo of the old man's shot was banging across the hollow.

He looked at me, eyebrows lifted. "Why didn't you shoot?"

I shrugged. I was finding it hard to believe that an old man—What was he? Seventy? Seventy-five?—shot quicker than a twenty-eight-year-old.

"Dead bird," the old man told his dog.

The setter had to search among the blackberry canes—she'd been screened by cover and hadn't marked the fall—but she found the grouse and brought it back. "Cockbird," the old man said. He held it to his chest and plucked from its tail a feather, which he poked into rotten wood atop the apple log. The feather stood like a brown-and-black banner. He pulled back his coat and slipped the bird into his game pouch, a roomy affair fashioned from a grain sack.

"That was a fine shot," I said.

"Thanks."

"Looks like you've made it before."

The old man nodded. "Once or twice."

We went on, the dog threading the alders before us. We had gone a hundred yards when the setter slowed on the edge of a small clearing. She crouched, sinking until her white-feathered tail touched the ground.

The old man motioned me in. A woodcock popped up on whistling wings—a sound as unnerving, in its own way, as a grouse's take-off—and as I adjusted to the slower game, shot, and saw the bird fall, the old man's gun barked twice. The dog retrieved my bird and carried it to her master. He sent her into the alders, where she found a second woodcock, and then he walked among the straight, gray trunks, bent down, and held up the other half of his double.

I wished I had seen the shooting. Judging from where the woodcock lay, they had gotten up well to one side and far apart; it had not been an easy double. I nodded, quite enough communication under the circumstances, as the old man gave me my game. He opened his shotgun, withdrew the spent cases, and reloaded. His shells were not plastic, but paper-wrapped.

"What did you say your name was?" I asked.

His shotgun shut with a dull click. The corners of his mouth turned up, and his eyes twinkled. "Deibler."

"Do you live around here?"

"Couple valleys north." He shot the words back over his shoulder; already he was following the setter into the brush.

The sun on the ridge outlined November-bare trees, and in the low spots frost-blackened weeds lay like matted fur. I trudged along with the old fellow.

Deibler. The more I thought, the surer I was he'd introduced himself by another name. Deibler was a solid central Pennsylvania name, and the old man spoke the local tongue, a dialect marked by inflection that rises and falls like the rough wooded hills; but if the name was different, the old man was more so. The clothes. The gun. The unhurried, take-it-as-it-comes posture of hunting. As if he'd stepped out of an era when game was more plentiful and time less in demand—and, therefore, fuller and more precious.

I was trying to make sense of this when I heard a grouse. The bird had flushed wild, on the other side of the old man, who had already spun and planted his feet when I looked. His body leaned toward the sound. He mounted his shotgun—a motion so fluid it almost escaped notice—swung, swung, and shot the instant the grouse entered a far opening in the trees. The bird thumped the ground. It was the kind of shot I have always wanted to make, and as I watched the old man stop his follow-through and lower his gun, I knew he could have hit it time and again.

Excitement filled his voice as he called the setter and directed her retrieve. I felt very much a spectator as he took the grouse and patted the dog on the head.

We were near a tumbledown house foundation, and the old man sat on the stones. He fanned the grouse's tail and stared at it, as if trying to read some message in the intricate play of chestnut, black, and gray. I broke my shotgun and sat beside him.

"You filled your limit in a hurry," I said.

"Did I? Oh—that's right. They only leave you take two these days." He ran thick fingers over the grouse's back feathers.

"How long have you been hunting?"

The old man squinted. "A long, long time. Since before this house fell down and before these fields were brush and briars."

"I guess you've killed a lot of birds."

"When I started hunting, a man dared shoot twenty grouse

161

in one day. I killed that many a good number of times."

He pulled a feather from the grouse's tail and wedged it between two stones.

"Yessir," he said, "one season I shot upwards of four hundred grouse and probably half that many woodcock. Shipped the grouse to Philadelphia for fifty cents apiece."

"When was that?"

The old man smiled, " 'Ninety-five."

It took me a moment to subtract. "Wait a minute. That'd make you . . ."

"All right, call it 'twenty-five."

I rested my chin on my hand and studied him. He had to be a liar. Then again, no man who shot the way he did needed to lie about anything.

"Where did you do your hunting?" I asked.

"Around here. And I spent a couple-three years up north, in that Black Forest country." He paused. "Are there birds up there yet?"

"Not many. The woods have grown up too much."

"You been to the Black Forest Inn?"

I nodded. "It burned down a couple of years ago."

He frowned. "Y'don't say?"

The hollow was darkening. Down in the big valley a train sounded a crossing. Odd, I thought. Here I am talking to this fellow—whoever he is—letting the day slip away, with half a grouse limit in my pouch.

No way, I thought, could the old man have hunted in 1895. And then I remembered the name: Detwiler.

"So, Mr. Detwiler," I said. "You've got me wondering about a lot of things."

"That's good. Keep on wondering."

"I'm wondering if you're a ghost." I almost laughed; the words just popped out of their own accord.

Mr. Detwiler spat between his boots. "A ghost. A real, honest-to-God haunt?"

I squirmed. "Not exactly. I mean, not the kind that lives in barns and old foundations and scares people."

He shook his head. "Nope."

"Well, then I'm stumped. I don't know who you are, or where you come from. Only that you handle a shotgun like no man I've ever seen."

He smiled. "That's all you have to know."

He stood and stretched, and the dog rose with a tired wag of her tail. Mist was starting down the hollow, and the apple trees looked broken-backed and full of secrets. A flight of blackbirds rushed over, and Mr. Detwiler glanced up, his face ruddy in the last light.

He looked at me. "You take care now."

I watched him move off. The sumacs and locusts closed around him. The tinkle of the setter's bell faded and vanished in the high, thin breeze.

I reached back and slipped a hand in my game pouch. My fingers touched the grouse, soft and cold. They closed around the long, thin bill of the woodcock. I looked at the talisman between the stones, and I knew I would search for grouse feathers many years to come.

Holding Infinity at Bay

If you want to know what wolverine sign looks like, or the color of the plumbeous kite, or where Pegasus reposes in the November sky, or how a sea nettle stings you, or what contact metamorphism is, or how to brew checkerberry tea—buy a field guide.

The best guides are the Peterson series, twenty-six squat, information-packed books with blue covers. The first one, *A Field Guide to the Birds*, was written by Roger Tory Peterson in 1934. Since then, it has sold over two million copies. Peterson, now the acknowledged dean of American birdwatchers, is editor of the entire Field Guide series, which is sponsored by the National Wildlife Federation, written by experts from various disciplines, and published by Houghton Mifflin Company, Boston.

The series exhibits considerable breadth. After subduing the birds ("Giving Field Marks of All Species Found East of the Rockies," says the subtitle), Peterson wrapped up the continent in 1941 with *A Field Guide to the Western Birds*. Guide number three was *Shells of the Atlantic and Gulf Coasts and the West Indies*, by Percy Morris. Alexander Klots of the American Museum of Natural History wrote the next, *Butterflies of North America, East of the Great Plains*. Other far-ranging additions include *Birds of Britain and Europe*, *Coral Reefs of the Caribbean and Florida*, *Rocky Mountain Wildflowers*, *The Atmosphere*, and *Stars and Planets*.

The butterfly book was the first field guide I owned. Outfitted with the book, a killing jar, and a long-handled green-mesh net—and, at home, panatela boxes and pins—I went hunting swallowtails. I heeded Klots's admonition not to "cavort madly across the landscape making roundhouse swings with the net." I learned to hold up the mesh bag after clapping it onto a sitting target: Invariably, the butterfly would flit up into the net. I learned how to transfer captives into the jar of chloroform. I caught swallowtails, tortoise shells, monarchs, questions marks, blues. Once I snagged a grackle with my net. I had a good look at him, and let him go.

The butterfly guide was first published almost thirty years ago, and it shares, with other field guides of its vintage, certain failings. Too many pictures in black and white, too few in color. The color illustrations are not as true-to-life as the reader might wish. In his acknowledgments, Klots cites Marjorie Statham's color illustrations and conveys regrets that "no system of reproduction can do full justice to her work."

Today, printing *can* do justice to fine illustrations. Advances in reproduction—as well as new information on many species—are two of the reasons why Roger Tory Peterson recently revised his bird book. For the fourth edition, marketed in 1980, Peterson redrew every bird. And he added more color. Where the old edition had 60 plates, 36 of them in color, the new book has 136 plates, nearly all of them in color.

Field guides depend heavily on illustrations. In a preface to one, Peterson writes, "A good drawing is usually more helpful in identification than a photograph. The latter is a record of a single moment, subject to the vagaries of chance, angle, light . . . On the other hand, a drawing is a composite of the artist's past experience, in which he can emphasize the important and edit out the irrelevant." Peterson wants his guides to be *used*—periodically he admonishes the reader not to leave them indoors—and to be *useful*. He instructs his experts to point out each subject's "badge, or identification tag, by which it may be known at a glance." Black arrows on the drawings indicate the salient marks: for the eastern kingbird, a white band on the tip of the tail; for the meadow fritillary butterfly, a squarish apex to the forewing; and so on, for lace-wings and lupines and bladdernoses and waterdogs and whelks.

A field guide that opened up a whole new world for me was *Reptiles and Amphibians of Eastern and Central North America*, by Roger Conant, former curator of reptiles at the Philadelphia Zoo. When I bought the guide, I didn't know the difference between a reptile and an amphibian. I soon learned that reptiles are armored with scales, shields, or plates—they are dry to the touch—while amphibians are sheathed in a moist skin. Young reptiles are miniature replicas of their parents; amphibians must pass through a larval stage, when they don't look anything like the adults. Reptiles include snakes, lizards, and turtles; salamanders, frogs, and toads are amphibians.

When I went camping, I always stuck the book in my pack. One day I backed a snake up against a rock. The snake was slender and black, with a white patch under its chin. It coiled, and switched the tip of its tail back and forth so fast it buzzed against the leaves. I consulted the guide. I identified the snake as a black racer, a hunter of rodents, small birds, other snakes, and insects. "Fights fiercely when cornered," Conant warned. I let the snake return to its business without capturing it for a better look. On another trip, I took the book down to the creek and began turning over stones. I uncovered a black-spotted, reddish-orange salamander that thrashed out of my grasp and darted away in the current (northern red salamander); a salamander whose tail was fully as long as its body (long-tailed salamander); and, under a stone on the bank, a brown salamander with a dark squiggle down its back (mountain dusky salamander; according to the field guide, it comes in a plethora of colors and patterns—sort of a catch-all for nondescript streamside salamanders.)

That day I also found a bewildering variety of insects beneath the rocks, and not long after I bought *A Field Guide to the Insects*, by Donald Borror and Richard White, a university professor and a research entomologist, respectively. *Insects* came out in 1970, and it is full of excellent illustrations. Borror and White

166

note that their guide is incomplete; they don't begin to have enough room for the eighty-eight thousand species of insects inhabiting America. The authors provide a pictorial key to help you find the order an insect belongs to. You can then make a stab at the family from detailed drawings in the text. In a few cases, notes lead you to the subfamily level, but you must turn to some more-specialized tome to come up with genus or species. No big problem for me at the moment: If I can tell an assassin bug from an ambush bug, that's enough.

While the insect realm is too vast for a single field guide, the world of ferns is not. Ferns, contends Peterson, form "a very satisfactory group if you would like to master one of the fields of natural science"—there are only about a hundred species in the entire Northeast. Boughton Cobb brought out *A Field Guide to the Ferns and Their Related Families* in 1956. Cobb, a successful business executive, wrote a brief, simple book. It is illustrated exclusively in black and white, an adequate scheme since ferns are basically green. After having used the guide to sort out some of the more common species, I find it hard to pass a patch of ferns without stopping.

Cobb doesn't tell you this, but you can eat the fiddleheads—the young, unfurling shoots—of many ferns. So says Lee Peterson, Roger Tory's son and author of *Edible Wild Plants*, number twenty-three in the series. The junior Peterson advises gathering the six- to eight-inch fiddleheads of bracken, our most abundant fern, and, after rubbing off their wooly covering, boiling the shoots for half an hour. They taste something like asparagus, he says. While most foraging books tell how to cook wild edibles, few pay attention to telling you where to gather the plants and how to identify them. Peterson's field guide, out in 1978, performs all three tasks. He may have hit upon the ideal illustration scheme: line drawings supplemented by a large selection of color photographs. Many of the drawings are his father's, reprinted from *Wildflowers* (1968) by Roger Tory Peterson and Margaret McKenny. Lee Peterson's book includes plants that can be cooked like garden vegetables, plants that yield candy, cereal, coffee, cold drinks, and seasonings, plants for pickling and making tea and grinding into flour. He shows many poisonous plants, those that might be mistaken for edible ones.

My favorite guide is *Animal Tracks*, by Olaus Murie. Murie was a field biologist for the U.S. Fish and Wildlife Service, and later director of The Wilderness Society. For many years he lived in the Jackson Hole country of Wyoming, where wild animals abound. Murie's drawings are simple line work sketched in all regions of the continent. They depict tracks in snow, sand, and mud; tracks revealing sequences of hunting, attacking, fleeing; droppings; nests and shelters; and signs of feeding. Notes accompany each illustration, and often an anecdote. From the wolverine: "I had shot a mountain sheep ram for a museum specimen. It was a bitterly cold winter day, and dusk was falling. There was not time to completely skin the animal and get back to my tent. I had seen wolverine tracks on the mountainside, and I knew what could happen to my specimen if I left it there. So I made a bargain with the wolverine . . . I partly skinned the ram back from the rear, laid the loose skin over the head, and left exposed the hind quarters and belly. . . Next morning I went back. There were wolverine tracks all around the carcass. Great chunks of the best meat had been taken, but my specimen, the skin and head, was untouched."

Animal Tracks is a rare field guide, one that you can read cover-to-cover like an ordinary book. Not that the other field guides are unremittingly dry reading. From *Atlantic Seashore*, by zoologist Kenneth Gosner: "Only a few marine invertebrates have vernacular names in common use, and the most interesting of these are indecent, having been applied by fishermen and other plain-seeing folk." From an entry on the osprey in *Birds' Nests*, by Hal Harrison: "John Steinbeck found 3 shirts, 1 bath towel, 1 arrow, and his rake in a nest in his garden." George Petrides's *Trees and Shrubs*, showing why he uses simple terminology: "The following description is concocted, but not unbelievably extreme: 'Stolonif-

168

erous shrub; leaves subcoriaceous, cuneate-ovate to lanceolate, denticulate, glabrescent; twigs terate, glaucous,' etc.''

Some of the Peterson guides are too technical. I can't read the maps in *Stars and Planets*. I stumble over the formulas and chemical tests in *Rocks and Minerals*. There are other problems. In many of the guides, color illustrations are grouped separately from the text. Segregating words and pictures will hold a book's price down, but it will not help the buyer who is forced to flip frantically back and forth between illustration and description while the insect that *may* be a grape leaf skeletonizer is windmilling through the leaves into the treetops above.

Flawed as they are, the Peterson guides are the best available. While some individual guides from competing series are better than their Peterson counterparts, no other group is as complete, as understandable, as utilitarian.

The main reason I use field guides, I suspect, is that I want to know names. I realize that this desire is not without danger. Leonard Rubinstein, a friend and a teacher of writing, says that names are necessary, profitable—and blinding. ''A newborn child must see an infinitely various, constantly shifting, kaleidoscopically colored field,'' he writes. ''An adult is separated by what he sees: what he sees is the seen and he is the seer. The baby is what he sees: infinity.

''Trying to encompass such a vision would drive an adult crazy. He must exclude most of it, reduce the rest of it, and organize the reduction into identities he can name. Each name holds the rest of infinity at bay.''

Three Incidents

August, the Absaroka Mountains, northeast of Togwotee Pass, Wyoming. On the third day of our trip we hike up Cub Creek, leave the trail, and follow a dry wash up the side of Crescent Mountain. In the wash, a gray, robin-size bird hops along in front of us, catching insects disturbed by our boots. It seizes a blue butterfly with white-edged wings, a cricket, and a grasshopper. The grasshopper's legs, twisted in the bird's beak, show stripes as orange as trout fins.

The bird stays behind when we reach the broad humped back of Crescent Mountain. Gray clouds float over from the west, casting huge shadows on the grass. Ribbons of snow lie across meadows blue with lupine. Green and black lichens blotch the flat brown rocks. Soon the clouds thicken and lightning fingers the mountain. As raindrops pelt down, we dig slickers out of our packs.

We hike north along the Continental Divide, picking our way over the wet rocks. The rain slackens for a moment and sunlight streams in from behind five angular ridges, each a shade of blue paler than the one in front. I slip off the pack, get out my camera, and take a picture. My companions keep walking. I photograph them—or, more accurately, their backpacks, blue and green rectangles about to disappear over a rise—with the pyramid of the Grand Teton, fifty miles west, in silhouette on the left horizon.

I pack the camera, hoist the pack—the straps cut into my shoulders, and I take time to adjust them—and set off after my

170

friends. Topping the rise, I expect to see them below. The flat is empty.

My stomach twitches. Two miles ahead is a narrow saddle connecting Crescent Mountain with the next peak to the north. We plan to camp on the saddle tonight. I hope to overtake my friends on the way.

I walk for an hour, but never catch up. Pikas, small mammals that look like guinea pigs, bleat from the rocks. Clouds swallow the mountains, wind gusts, rain slants down. I stop and unpack a whistle. I always carry it in the high country; I have never used it before. I blow three blasts, listen carefully, and hear no answering notes—only the ventriloquial, sheep-like calls of the pikas.

My shoulders are sore and my legs feel liquid. I keep walking. The rain lets up and the clouds part, revealing a landscape that is totally foreign to the mental map I have been following. Sharp-edged mountains and deep green valleys, a blue pyramid peeking over the skyline on my right. I stare at the pyramid for several seconds before recognizing it as the Grand Teton. It was on my left when I took the picture of my friends.

I turn, shucking off the pack and letting it thump to the ground. I dig out a compass and a topographic map, unfold the map, hold it down with my boots, and lay the compass on it. I realize I am at least three miles south of the saddle, close to where we followed the dry wash up onto Crescent Mountain. The rain picks up again. The Grand Teton disappears, and all the other mountains. Clutching the compass, I get moving.

The way we divided the load, I am in poor shape to travel alone. I have food, but it is dehydrated stuff that requires cooking, and I have no stove, pots, or pans. A sleeping bag, but no tent—the bag is goose down, and if it gets wet it will not keep me warm. I carry the only set of maps in the group: We left a second set at the trailhead by mistake. One of my companions hiked this mountain and camped on the saddle two years ago; he will have to lead the others to the spot without a map. If he cannot find the saddle and they tent somewhere else—or if I fail to reach the camp before dark—I am on my own. My mind reviews the procedure. Get down to timberline. Find water. Crawl under a windfall spruce or a rock ledge. Build a fire. Eat something—cook it in a cup. Put on every stitch of wool, and over it my raincoat, and sit out the night. Pray for clear weather. In the morning, climb up high, find the saddle, and wait.

I hike north, checking the compass every hundred yards. My thigh muscles ache, and the pack's waistband chafes my hips. I try to walk fast enough to reach the saddle before dark, slow enough to keep from falling. The light dims; lupines sway blue heads; the smell of wet wool rises from my collar.

I top three rises, each time telling myself, out loud, that the tents will be there. Nothing. I begin to wonder if I will recognize the saddle if my friends are not camped on it.

I follow an elk trail to the top of another crest. Far below, on a narrow pass, sit a pair of tents. They look like brown jewels in the grass. Three people squat in front of the tents. One of them looks at the ridge. My friends jump up, waving and shouting. Their cries barely reach me against the wind.

Dawn is early for a grouse hunter to be out. Shivering, I tug on a pair of deerskin gloves, stretch my shoulders, load the shotgun. All the fall colors are gone. Sodden leaves cover the ground, with grains of snow collected against their ribs. Leaves, bare trees, blackberry canes, rocks, grapevines—all look dull in the dim light, as if coated with dust.

I walk slowly toward a pine. I peer among the branches. The grouse will not have left their roosts yet.

A crow calls a long way off. I smell wet dirt. All around, the leaves have been scuffed away from the ground—turkeys looking for fallen grapes and hawthorn fruits.

I hunt up the hollow, keeping where I can see and swing the shotgun, a few feet uphill from the thicket that encloses the little stream. I work to the head of the hollow, hunt around the leaf-choked spring, and start back on the other side.

172

Five yelps come from the brush partway down the hollow. I stop and sink to a crouch. More yelps. A young turkey separated from its flock. When the bird calls again, I decide to hunt toward it on my way out of the hollow. I have friends who hunt turkeys, and I smile at the prospect of telling them I shot one while gunning for grouse.

The ground muffles my steps. The bird keeps calling in plaintive, ascending notes that change in volume, as if it were facing first in one direction, then another. I slip forward. The calling comes from the base of a vine-covered bush about fifty feet away. My eyes strain.

A dark, narrow shape flaps up and down—the wing of a turkey taking off. I press the gun toward my shoulder, thumb the safety off. Something stops me. There is no sound with the flapping.

As I stare, the flapping becomes waving, and a face coalesces behind the vines.

I drop to my knees, open the shotgun's action, and lay the gun on the leaves; my heart bangs against my ribs. A man stands and extracts himself from the vines. He is wearing a tattered brown coat, brown pants, and a green hat. Gray stubble covers his face. He walks over to me and looks down. I see in his eyes that he has no idea how close I came. He tells me that a flock of turkeys was broken up here yesterday afternoon.

He wanders back to his stand, and I leave the hollow. I shoot a grouse that afternoon, a beautiful snap shot of a speeding bird, and I find no pleasure in it at all. My uncle in Wyoming was supposed to have killed his partner many years ago while hunting elk. I never could ask him if he really did it. He had bottles all over the place—in the tool box on his baler, under an old tarp, behind the air compressor. Some years he hunted, some years he didn't.

I sit against a tree. The sun has not cleared the mountain. The air is cold and still. I can barely hear the scuffle of a hunter who walked past a minute before, just after first light. Dull booms, like the slamming of distant doors, echo off the hills.

Before I see the deer I hear it, a rustling from behind a patch of mountain laurel. A buck steps out. His body is big and angular, his chest deep, his neck thick. He holds his head down, white tines of antlers poking high above his ears.

The buck raises his head and looks around. My pulse races. I shoulder the rifle. I know I should wait. The buck's body is blocked by a tree. Soon he will take another step, giving me a body shot, an easy shot. I ease the safety off and settle the scope's reticle on his neck. I touch the trigger, squeeze it, pull.

The trigger will not budge. I thumb for the safety—it is only partway down. I push it the rest of way. The buttstock slams my shoulder, the rifle roars.

I know instantly what happened: My finger was on the trigger when I pushed the safety off. The shot went over the deer's back. He stands, looking at me. I bolt another shell into the chamber. At the action's clash, he whirls and runs, bounding back the way he came, tail waving with each leap. I stand, swing the rifle, and aim ahead of him at an opening in the trees. Before he reaches the opening he turns and runs directly away. I do not shoot.

I lean back into the tree. My stomach is knotted, and my hands clench the gun.

I sit out the morning and return to camp at noon. A spike buck is hanging from a pole between two trees. The buck I missed was almost twice as big. Another hunter asks if I shot, and I shake my head no. He says he heard a shot from the direction of my stand, one shot, and expected to see me dragging a deer. I lie to him. I tell him someone else shot.

I sling the rifle and start off toward a new stand. My stomach is tight and queasy. I stop, go back. I tell the hunter how I shot at the buck and missed.

Lord and Master of June

Clark Shiffer, a short, round-faced man with a straw hat and hip boots, stands in water to his thighs, staring out over the spatter-dock. In his hands is a long-handled net. He crouches slightly, like a sentry who has just heard a noise.

"That's *Anax longipes*," he says to me. "Oh, wonderful! He's back again this year." He wipes sweat from his nose. "Ah, boy, *longipes* is really whipping around here now. He's going to make a fatal turn, and I'm going to get him. And look—that's *Anax junius*, and over there is *Libellula pulchella*."

Sunlight sparkles on Ten Acre Pond. Waxwings trill, killdeer titter, a bullfrog growls. Suddenly Shiffer swoops his net through the air and traps a pocket of gauze over the rim. He clasps the netting with his left hand, reaches in with his right, and extracts a dragonfly. Pinning its wings between his index and middle fingers, he turns it in the light. The dragonfly's thorax is pale green, a bubble of a hide through which organs glimmer. Each bulging olive eye reflects a sunny hexagon. The three-inch turquoise tail is segmented like bamboo.

"*Anax junius*," Shiffer says. He slips the dragonfly into a glassine envelope—its wings kazoo against the paper. He reaches in and turns its head to one side. "If you forget to turn the head, it'll chew its legs off. Ruins its value as a specimen."

He tucks the envelope in his shirt pocket, shakes out the net, and looks over the pond. "Now for *longipes*," he says.

Earlier, I had visited Shiffer's study, a small, dark room smelling of mothballs. Two collecting nets leaned in a corner. A stereomicroscope cast a long shadow in the light from a goosenecked lamp. On shelves sat funnels, forceps, bottles of clear liquid, hand lenses, notebooks, pens, inkwells, maps, rubber boots, ice chests, and four dozen brown rectangular boxes. One box lay open on the desk. Shiffer's bald head bobbed above it as he flipped through the plastic-wrapped index cards inside.

"Sorry about the smell," he said. "Without the mothballs, dermestid beetles would reduce my dragonflies to dust. Those things can squeeze through a window screen."

He pulled out a card. Under the plastic, a dragonfly lay on its side, legs tucked up, long slender wings folded over its back.

"Note the two pairs of wings," Shiffer said. "The front wings beat independently of the hind ones, letting the critter do some pretty amazing things. It can hit twenty-five miles per hour with ease. It can stop on a dime. It can hover and fly backwards, like a hummingbird." He pushed a button on the microscope and slid the specimen into the circle of light. I bent to the eyepieces.

Magnified twenty times, the wings reflected red, green, and blue highlights. Their surface was knit into a complex mosaic by hundreds of straight black ribs forming triangles, trapezoids, pentagons, hexagons, and octagons.

"Like chicken wire, huh?" Shiffer said. "The black lines are veins. Blood flowing through the larger ones helps keep the airfoils stiff. The solid patches on the leading edge of each wing are the pterostigmata—blood reservoirs that act as counterweights to stabilize the insect in flight.

"The head also helps with balancing. It sits on a flexible neck, so it always stays level, no matter what the body is doing. Like this." He spread his arms, pumped them, rotated his hips. His head, gleaming in the light from the desk lamp, never moved.

I looked back into the microscope at the iridescent wings. When I nudged the dragonfly with a finger, a bristled, barbed, and plated monster leaped into view.

"Look at the eyes," Shiffer said. "See the facets? Each facet is a sensor. A big dragonfly like *Anax junius* has about twenty-eight thousand facets in each eye. Even a small dragonfly—one of the damselflies, say—has seven thousand. I've made a sudden move and had dragonflies take off twenty, thirty feet away.

"Dragonflies see a lot, but they don't see everything. My son Tom is probably the only person in the world to be hit smack in the middle of the forehead by a *Somatochlora incurvata*. It was a female being hotly pursued by a male across the leatherleaf."

Shiffer touched a probe to the legs, which crooked forward like six slender iron rods. Each presented a row of sharp spikes and ended in a two-pronged claw.

"A dragonfly takes its prey on the wing," he said. "It bunches its legs together into a basket. If it scoops up a small insect—like a mosquito—the front legs transfer the prey to the mouth, and the dragonfly chews it down without missing a wingbeat. If it catches something larger, a bumblebee or a moth, it may have to land. Dragonflies also eat each other. I once saw *Anax junius* seize *Cordulia shurtleffi*. Before they could hit the ground, *Anax longipes* grabbed both of them. I flopped my net on the whole bunch."

Shiffer thumbed through the index cards. "I'll be darned," he said. "The last time I caught *longipes* was five years ago."

A thin layer of clouds has slipped in front of the sun. The land shimmers with toadlets—pea-size, dun amphibians emerging from the pond by the thousands. Shiffer and I tiptoe through the throng, the toads scattering wildly. We slog into the shallows, and the water molds our hips boots to our legs.

"Note the sudden paucity of dragonflies," Shiffer says. "Most of them disappear as soon as the sun goes behind a cloud. Nobody knows just why. Maybe they're afraid of rain—they have a hard time flying then. Maybe they need the sun for orienting, or for keeping warm."

To stay active, a dragonfly has to keep its body temperature steady, Shiffer tells me. Damselflies, which perch a lot, angle

177

toward the sun to soak up just the right amount of heat. Steady fliers beat their wings to warm up, glide to cool down. Big dragonflies like *Anax junius* vent heat by circulating more blood through their abdomens.

The clouds break up, and the pond begins to glare. Suddenly dragonflies are everywhere. Around my hips flicker tiny green-and-blue damselflies. A white-faced dragonfly perches on a milk jug mired in the shallows. *Anax junius* sashays above the weeds; I lift a hand, and it zips away.

"*Junius* is a common species," says Shiffer. "It lives in China and Kamchatka and Hawaii and Mexico. Most people call it the green darner. The Latin name means 'Lord and Master of June.' "

Dragonflies, Shiffer says, were flying through the primordial swamps millions of years before dinosaurs arrived. Among insects, only the mayflies, and maybe the roaches, are older. One dragonfly race died out: giants with two-foot wingspans. The species living today have not changed in 150 million years, judging from the unaltered patterns of their wing veins.

Somewhere along the line, dragonflies settled on a bizarre love-making position. The male darts ahead of the female and clasps her neck with the tip of his tail. As they fly in tandem, the female curls her own tail-tip—bearing her sex organs—to join the male's genitals, beneath his tail near the thorax. Locked in a misshapen wheel, they fly or perch until sperm is transferred. The males of at least one species make sure their own genes are advanced: They use their penises to scrape out sperm deposited by an earlier mating.

The sexes rendezvous at ponds, puddles, streams, and swimming pools. Males return to the same spot each day, defending it against other males. Or, they patrol—flying, stopping, looking, moving, searching for females.

"Hold still," Shiffer says.

A big blue dragonfly plies the shore, heading our way. Twenty feet in front of us, a green darner rises to meet it. Wings chitter as the combatants spin about. Quickly they separate, and the blue dragonfly continues toward us.

178

Mouth twisted and eyes intent, Shiffer lets it pass. His net sweeps from behind, overtaking, engulfing, snapping shut with a wrist-flick. The dragonfly rustles in the gauze.

Shiffer grins. *"Aeschna mutata."*

The dragonfly's eyes are liquid blue. Azure stripes slant across its body. Its tail is blue on black, like an Arizona sky above a new asphalt road.

"This is rare," he says. "Ten Acre Pond is the only place in Pennsylvania where *mutata* can be taken in number. The females like the spatterdock, that green floating plant with the yellow flower. They lay their eggs in the flower stems."

He sets the dragonfly on the rim of the net. It raises its abdomen and rubs a front leg across one eye. It whirs into the air, circles the pond, lifts above the bordering trees, and vanishes.

"If you think he's colorful," says Shiffer, "wait'll you see *longipes.*"

On a blade of sedge at the margin of the pond, a squat brown insect is frozen in an attitude of climbing. I kneel for a closer look, and find that the insect is only a skin. The translucent husk is parted down the back, with white threads dangling from the slit.

"That's a dragonfly skin," says Shiffer, eating a peanut butter-and-jelly sandwich. "Everybody knows what a dragonfly is, but who knows that it's already spent three quarters of its life underwater? Those white strands on the back are tubes that helped the nymph change from a water-breathing to an air-breathing creature."

Shiffer opens the ice chest, where a dozen glassine envelopes hold numbed captives, and digs out a 7-Up. He pops and pockets the tab, takes a swallow. His gaze is riveted on a half-dozen red spots skittering at the end of the pond.

"It must be strange on the bottom," he says. "The nymphs hide in the muck, feeding on each other and whatever else happens by. They have a lower lip with a couple of hooks on the end"—he holds his hand, palm-up and two fingers extended, under his chin—"which they shoot out to grasp prey"—his hand leaps forward and back. He pops the last bite of sandwich into his mouth. "They're death on mosquito wrigglers. Eat 'em by the thousands. The big larvae, like *longipes* or *junius*, even eat small fish.

"A nymph molts about a dozen times, until there's a real dragonfly under that skin. Then it climbs up on the bank and squeezes out of its wrapper. Blood and air pump through the wings and abdomen, and both expand. After a while the insect takes off. Its body is soft, and it can't fly very well. A dragonfly at this stage is called a teneral—birds get a lot of them. The survivors harden over the next few days. They have about a month to mate, and to lay eggs if they're female, before they die."

Shiffer drains off his drink and picks up the net. He walks into the water, wades to a narrow inlet, and crouches.

Longipes flash over the pond, sleek, with pod-like, jade thoraxes and gleaming, blood-red tails. They weave over the spatterdock, streak across open water. They hover, dip, break away, hover again.

"Dragonflies are the toughest insects to capture," Shiffer calls over his shoulder. "You can't go running after them waving your net. You can't swipe at them from the front—they see the net and dodge it. You have to learn their habits. You concentrate on an individual, watch his flight pattern, see where he interacts with other dragonflies, where he looks for a mate. Pretty soon you're inside his head."

A *longipes* approaches. It decelerates, sidles around just out of range, and zooms away. Shiffer watches it go, ignoring a yellowjacket bobbing an inch from his nose.

"Some collectors," he says, "knock them out of the air with dust-shot from a .22."

For the next several hours we wade the shoreline, setting up ambushes. Deerflies orbit our heads. Newts hang in the murk like sleepy alligators. The big, red-tailed *longipes*—five or six of them are on the pond—fly over and around us, tempting Shiffer but never giving him a chance to strike.

During a lull, he talks about his hobby.

"An odonatologist," he says, "is one who studies order Odonata. I'm one of three serious odonatologists in Pennsylvania, and the other two are married to each other. In the whole world, there are maybe three hundred—at least that's how many belong to Societas Internationalis Odonatologica. The society meets every other year to give papers, trade specimens, and go collecting. I made it to the last two sessions, in Gainesville, Florida, and in Montreal. This year's meeting is over in Switzerland. I'd like to go, but I can't afford it."

Shiffer says about half of the odonatologists are university biologists. The others include highway engineers, bankers, farmers, mailmen, electricians, businessmen. Shiffer is Herpetology and Endangered Species Coordinator for the Pennsylvania Fish Commission. He first became interested in dragonflies in 1963, when taking a college entomology course. Today he has fifty-three hundred specimens. Other odonatologists have amassed collections of several hundred thousand.

"A lot of odonatologists end up divorced," Shiffer says. "They develop such an intense fixation that they neglect their wives and children. Marriages fall apart, families dissolve. It's never over for the collector: Once he's got a good series of odonates, he shifts to the hover flies, or the mayflies.

"Mary thinks my hobby is a little odd, but she puts up with it. I guess she realizes I am compelled to pursue facts."

Sunlight glancing off the water illuminates old stumps, beer cans, and the emergent, heart-shaped leaves of the spatterdock. Over the leaves fly hundreds of bright dragonflies.

I have the net. The handle is wrapped with adhesive tape, the gauze grass-stained. It has a nice heft to it, and makes a satisfying whoosh through the air.

I try to zero in on a single dragonfly. I pick out a big blue flier—*Aeschna mutata*, I believe—far across the water and coming my way. It grows in my field of vision and passes within range. I strike. It lifts just enough to clear the net, drops back, flies on.

I have let the netting trail in the water and must now flag it back and forth to dry.

"Use more wrist and swing from behind," Shiffer tells me. "Hey, see that dragonfly dipping its abdomen in the pond? That's *Leucorrhinia intacta* ovipositing. Each dip washes off a dozen or so eggs." Shiffer sloshes around, the water rising near his boot tops. "I'm going to try for a picture. Catch *longipes* if you can."

I crouch deeper, and find that the lower perspective reduces the glare and lets me pick out the dragonflies more quickly. I spot a *longipes* over deep water. It cruises back and forth, a little closer with each pass. It snicks past, out of range but close enough for me to glimpse red legs dangling and eyes wrapping the head like a helmet. It heads straight for Shiffer.

"*Longipes!*" I yell.

Shiffer whips off his hat. "I see him! I'll slap him down if he comes close enough!" His bald head glistens. "I'm not above doing that, you know."

The dragonfly stops between us. It rises, rocking slightly, and flies away over the trees.

The sun is low in the west. Shiffer says we should call it quits; his wife had supper ready an hour ago. We fetch the ice chest and climb the clay bank, cross a band of oaks, and walk the gravel road to Shiffer's station wagon. Sitting on the tailgate, we tug at our boots.

Shiffer stops and looks up. Silhouetted against the deep blue sky are dragonflies, a dozen of them, dipping and darting, flying at stall speed.

"That's a feeding swarm," he says. I hand him the net.

Fetch

It is dawn, an April day.

I stand beside a stream fed by two springs welling from jumbled sandstone rocks. The stream rushes among the rough rocks and pitches, white, into a dark pool. It slips over more rocks, slick, shiny, smooth, and flows swiftly down the hollow.

I stand shivering, wondering why I am here. Everything—the stream, the mountains, the surrounding trees—seems an amalgam of many places I have known: familiar, yet strange; comforting, and somehow disquieting.

On each side of the stream a mountain rises a thousand feet into deep-blue sky. Each slope is covered with gray, leafless trees, each is a mirror image of the other. Nestled between the mountains, dwarfed by them, the stream hollow is crowded and full of the scent of damp leaves and rotting wood.

Spring has not yet climbed this high. Buds are tight on beech limbs arching across the stream, and snow rims the shady side of boulders. Still, there are signs of the season to come: Tight-whorled heads of mandrake poke green and maroon from the humus, white flowers show among fern fiddleheads, and birds call tentatively from the shadows.

April. The month of my birth and accumulating years. As a child, I held it in reverence. It was a point on the wheel of seasons, a time of renewal on which to anchor the rest of the year. In April in my hometown, men hoed gardens and women hung laundry on outdoor lines, and I watched them, child-quiet and proud, as they used my month.

Now I walk along the mountain stream. On rocks, sandpipers dip and scuttle. A woodpecker drums a hollow tree.

All around, trees grow thick and tall—feathery hemlocks, gray-barked beech, arrow-straight cherries. From the top of one comes a soft chuckling; I look in time to see a crow leap from a branch. The bird lands in a nearby sapling. It cocks its head in my direction, springs suddenly into the air, and flaps downstream.

In the hollow, the air is cold and clear. It harks back memories of other mornings in the mountains, some here and others far to the west and east. Mornings when we stood in ragged shadows, when the glaciers were cast in pink and mist filled the valleys below. I do not recall them as distinct, separate mornings, but as a bright band of primal time that slowed the slide of life.

I hear cawing and look up. The crow is back, flying above the trees; its wings flash black and silver. I track its flight through an open glade and find myself no longer hemmed in by mountains, but among wooded hills. I stand stock still. I have no idea how long I've been walking, or why the mountains vanished. Somehow, my mind has gone awry: I sense my thoughts are not to be trusted, but the pure light soothes, and I am lulled by the sight of greening shrubs and the sound of birds singing.

The sun—a moment ago blocked by a mountain—is high in the sky. It shines on the brown hills, where here and there a cottage roof glints among the trees. The stream, too, is changed: It runs broad, full of crooks and bends, pooling below mossy rocks. In a glade near the water sit grackles, black, yellow-eyed, sleek as fish. Some sing rasping songs; others fly in pairs, trailing long strands of grass from their beaks.

The grackles scatter.

My eye picks up a hawk streaking low over the ground. It sweeps up into a tree, lands, bobs its head. It takes off again immediately and darts past me. As I turn, I see its prey: a flicker, crouched on the ground.

184

The hawk strikes the flicker. Both birds roll, but the hawk rights itself first and bites the flicker at the back of the skull. The hawk's narrow wings form a mantle over the flicker's body. It begins to tear feathers from the pale breast.

I'm only paces away, but the hawk doesn't seem bothered. It tears the flicker in pieces, bolting the flesh. I take a step forward—still no reaction. On the accipiter's chest is a spot of blood, like a medal.

I turn and walk again, leaving the glade and making my way along the water's edge, where feeding fish dimple the surface of the stream. The quick, rolling wingbeats of a drumming grouse strike my ears; I hear squirrels chasing in the leaves, scrabbling up bark. One pops around the side of an oak, so close I can see its whiskers. It is all soft motion—fluid limbs, curling tail—as it swaps ends and vanishes behind the trunk.

Red-winged blackbirds flock over in a rush of brown and black, and doves pass in straight, purposeful flight. At my feet are pale-sepaled anemones, twigs, shoots of grass.

I squat and feel the world around me. For the moment, it is enough to sit and sense, to shrug off all thought of purpose and future, simply to be. Like the snail leaving a mother-of-pearl trail across a stump. Like the flowers of maples spreading a red haze through the woods. Like the wind.

On the wind I hear a crow, commanding attention with its incessant call. The bird lands in the top of a hickory, from which it can spy in any direction. Other crows feed in a new-plowed field, hopping among the furrows. The crow in the hickory sees me, sounds a general alarm, and the flock takes to the air, streaming into the next field, where they settle with much wing-flapping and discussion.

I see now how the woods have given way to farmland—rolling, steady, sedate. Settled into the land are stone houses, white barns, corncribs. The stream is broad; stepping stones show dry above the water, and thick, mottled branches of sycamores cast shadows on the green surface.

This time the sudden change of scenery doesn't jar me; I see it as the pattern of this April day.

I sit and rest under the trees, where the water makes a low, steady rush. Squinting at the sun, I realize that through the morning and now, into the afternoon, there have been no clouds—just a blue sky changing in hue and saturation with the sun's passage.

I ponder the advantages of being a sometime-child. Of being able, when the occasion asks it, to shed my adult skin and stand raw and bright to receive the world. The feeling lets me leave myself, as a metamorphosing cicada leaves its transparent husk clinging to a tree.

Movement, in a field, demands my attention. A fox, curiously two-toned: Its head and shoulders are dazzling orange, its back, sides, and tail are pale and blond—like the sun at dawn, the sun at midday. The dull, bushy fur on the fox's hindquarters is the unshed remnant of a pelt bleached by sun and snow the winter past.

The fox trots by, and I note its small, black nose, panting tongue, triangular ears, and black, spindly legs.

I stand, lightheaded. The sun is lower now; if I could force my eyes to stare, I think I might detect its downward crawl.

Here the path is beaten smooth. Muddy spots have captured tracks of deer and raccoons. The path takes me by the stream, wide and sluggish.

Behind, the water reflects blue sky; ahead, it shimmers under the sun. I follow the path until I find water on both sides, where the stream bends back on itself. The land is grown up with cattails and reed grass. A bittern stands on the bank, its bill turned up like a stem. The trail turns and backtracks out of the oxbow.

The land is neat and prosperous no more. Fields choke with hawthorn and sumac, apple trees bend scarred limbs to the ground. In the grass lies a scatter of blue feathers, where a jay died under talon or claw.

I find myself striding out, picking up speed. My legs hurry me on, the day grants no more time.

A woodcock flies from an aspen stand, long-beaked and squatty; a rabbit flees through the brush, and a band of sparrows. The path winds among crumbling foundations covered with vines, where discarded metal—gears, wheels, chains—rusts in the weeds. A deer trail intersects my path, scattered with elliptical, black droppings, gray where mold is breaking them down. All around, the earth is greening, budding, shooting forth, rotting, returning, and re-emerging.

The sun casts long shadows and lends a ruddy glow to the aspens. The day is almost done, and I realize I have seen no other travelers, no wanderers like myself. The path descends, through gaunt locust trees. A whippoorwill—brown, round-winged, seemingly beakless—flutters from the ground like a huge moth; I scarcely give it a glance.

I stumble, confused; the path branches three ways and I hurry down the middle route. Questions swirl inside my mind, refusing to take shape.

The path ends in a bog, where tree frogs shriek and shriek.

I stand, panting. My throat is dry but I fear drinking from the bog or the dark river that slips slowly past. Across the water the far shore is low and unbroken, a brushstroke across paper; ahead, the bog reflects the purpling sky.

Through the sky flies a bird. It flies with slow, regular wingbeats, and is so far away that it seems to pulsate—to diminish in size, then expand—with each stroke. A long time passes before the bird is close enough to identify: a crow. It quarters over the river, showing me the clasped beak, the tucked feet, the fingerlike wingtips.

The crow flares its wings, pumps them to decelerate, and lands in a snag on an island in the stream. It begins to call, the monotonous caws barely audible above the shrieking frogs.

The land is dark. The sky is green and blue on the horizon, deep blue above. I sit clumsily, drained of strength, and breathe the dank air.

The crow stops calling.

Silently it leaves the tree and beats its way through the air. Black and silent it flies in the sky, higher and higher. I crane my neck. The crow is a black spot, it fades, it is gone—then it clears the earth's shadow and is bright beyond imagination against the vaulting sky.